I0411234

Every day is a new opportunity. You can build on yesterday's success or put its failures behind and start over again. That's the way life is, with a new game every day, and that's the way baseball is.

Bob Feller

Do what you love to do and give it your very best. Whether it's business or baseball, or the theater, or any field. If you don't love what you're doing and you can't give it your best, get out of it. Life is too short. You'll be an old man before you know it.

Al Lopez

People ask me what I do in winter when there's no baseball. I'll tell you what I do. I stare out the window and wait for spring.

Rogers Hornsby

Baseball is like a poker game. Nobody wants to quit when he's losing; nobody wants you to quit when you're ahead.

Jackie Robinson

Baseball was, is and always will be to me the best game in the world.

Babe Ruth

Baseball is ninety percent mental and the other half is physical.

Yogi Berra

Love is the most important thing in the world, but baseball is pretty good, too.

Yogi Berra

Baseball is a team game but, at the same time, it's a very lonely game: unlike in soccer or basketball, where players roam around, in baseball everyone has their little plot of the field to tend. When the action comes to you, the spotlight is on you but no one can help you.

Chad Harbach

The way I figured it, I was even with baseball and baseball with me. The game had done much for me, and I had done much for it.

Jackie Robinson

There is really a je ne sais quoi about turkey cooking - the air of festivity, the family squabbles, the constant basting - that does not apply to the turkey breast, which is, really, a convenience of food... A turkey without seasonal angst is like a baseball game without a national anthem, a winter without snow, a birthday party without candles.

Laurie Colwin

There are three types of baseball players: Those who make it happen, those who watch it happen and those who wonder what happens.

Tommy Lasorda

Baseball is a lot like life. It's a day-to-day existence, full of ups and downs. You make the most of your opportunities in baseball as you do in life.

Ernie Harwell

February is always a bad month for TV sports. Football is

gone, basketball is plodding along in the annual midseason doldrums, and baseball is not even mentioned.

Hunter S. Thompson

Baseball is the only field of endeavor where a man can succeed three times out of ten and be considered a good performer.

Ted Williams

There are only two seasons - winter and Baseball.

Bill Veeck

One of the beautiful things about baseball is that every once in a while you come into a situation where you want to, and where you have to, reach down and prove something.

Nolan Ryan

Little League baseball is a very good thing because it keeps the parents off the streets.

Yogi Berra

In an individual sport, yes, you have to win titles. Baseball's different. But basketball, hockey? One person can control the tempo of a game, can completely alter the momentum of a series. There's a lot of great individual talent.

Kobe Bryant

You can't sit on a lead and run a few plays into the line and just kill the clock. You've got to throw the ball over the damn plate and five the other man his chance. That's why baseball is the greatest game of them all.

Earl Weaver

I don't know of any other organization that's raised more money than golf has, because if you are a baseball player, you're a football player, you're a hockey player, if you're just a businessman, and you want to raise some money for a charity, what do they do? They have a golf tournament. They have a golf outing, and they go out and they do it.

Lee Trevino

Normal people have an incredible lack of empathy. They have good emotional empathy, but they don't have much empathy for the autistic kid who is screaming at the baseball game because he can't stand the sensory overload.

Or the autistic kid having a meltdown in the school cafeteria because there's too much stimulation.

Temple Grandin

You know that a given in life in human nature, is that at a sporting event, a baseball game, a football game, you never introduce a politician, is because he'll be booed. I don't care if he's the most beloved person in the world, its part of the game.

Mark Russell

It took me seventeen years to get three thousand hits in baseball. I did it in one afternoon on the golf course.

Hank Aaron

There is no room in baseball for discrimination. It is our national pastime and a game for all.

Lou Gehrig

Growing up, I looked up to major league baseball players, and now these young women have amazing, incredible women all across the board, from swimming to gymnastics to softball to basketball. It is incredible how far women have come and women in sports have come.

Jennie Finch

Baseball is a slow, boring, complex, cerebral game that doesn't lend itself to histrionics. You 'take in' a baseball game, something odd to say about a football or basketball game, with the clock running and the bodies flying.

Charles Krauthammer

Baseball is drama with an endless run and an ever-changing cast.

Joe Garagiola

There has always been a saying in baseball that you can't make a hitter, but I think you can improve a hitter. More than you can improve a fielder. More mistakes are made hitting than in any other part of the game.

Ted Williams

Every baseball crowd, like every theatre audience, has its own distinctive attitude and atmosphere.

Bill Veeck

Not bragging by any means, but I could have done a lot of other stuff as far as working in films go and working in television... I had chances to do that stuff, but I like baseball, I really do.

Bob Uecker

You can keep going on and on about the interactions of people, which makes it a great drama and great event ,and you'll always hold that special, but if you're looking at a baseball moment, the feeling you get when you win the World Series by far exceeds anything else in the game that you're able to do.

Cal Ripken, Jr.

As a supporter of the Prostate Cancer Foundation and their Home Run Challenge program, I am extremely grateful for the valuable partnerships and relationships built with Major League Baseball and our affiliates.

Joe Torre

For me, baseball is more comparable to chess than it is to

hockey.

Jeff Garlin

Baseball is my escape. The sights, the sounds, the way the park smells. There is truly no place I would rather be than at a game.

Alyssa Milano

There's a bigger difference now than when I first got into professional baseball because that was before guaranteed contracts, before there was a lot of money, so it was mostly survival. You had more competition.

Tony La Russa

I have a love of baseball and a love of music.

Jason Aldean

You have to go understand that life and baseball is littered with all kinds of obstacles and problems along the way. You have to learn how to overcome them to be successful in life.

Dave Winfield

You shouldn't have any betting in the locker room at all, whether it's baseball or it's horses. You can't beat the horses. You can't beat any kind of gambling because they have the odds.

George Steinbrenner

I am convinced that God wanted me to be a baseball player.

Roberto Clemente

Many baseball fans look upon an umpire as a sort of necessary evil to the luxury of baseball, like the odor that follows an automobile.

Christy Mathewson

You should never wear a baseball cap when working in close quarters in the attic: You never see that beam above you!

Alex Trebek

I knew that I was a gay boy fairly early; what was interesting to me was that my mother didn't know. She made me play baseball - I had no desire to do that. I said, 'Mom, I don't like direct sunlight, I don't like bugs, I don't like grass, and I'd rather be in the house playing with your fabric samples.'

Nate Berkus

One reason outfielders don't have stronger arms might be they don't practice as much as we did. Most teams today don't take outfield practice. Another reason is baseball has to compete with other sports now - basketball, football, soccer - for the better athletes that might have more skills and stronger arms.

Al Kaline

My mum lives in Boston; she's famous for teaching wushu and t'ai chi. So from when I was young, my mum and aunt were like: 'You're training; you're not playing baseball or football.' Training every day was normal. Later, when I was almost a teenager, Bruce Lee became my idol.

Donnie Yen

I think that when people join clubs as simple as a sorority or a fraternity, a football team, a baseball team, it's just - you want to be in a group. You want to be around people, you want to be with people.

Theo Rossi

I played baseball up until my freshman year of high school. That was my main sport. I played third base.

Macklemore

I love baseball. The game allowed me the influence to impact kids in a positive way. This gives me a chance to talk to some social issues.

Cal Ripken, Jr.

Right now I like baseball, hockey and tennis players. And horseback riders.

Martina Hingis

I just want to play baseball.

David Ortiz

The beautiful thing about baseball is that anything can happen. It's like life in that way. As soon as you think you have it all figured out, something happens that makes you realize - you know nothing. The only thing that's guaranteed is that it will be an exciting ride.

Alyssa Milano

My main objective is to prepare candidates for professional baseball; however, the majority of our graduates will go home as much better qualified amateurs.

Jim Evans

I took a huge risk leaving baseball, because I was predicted to play in the big leagues. I'm kind of a prototypical second baseman.

Russell Wilson

The game is just, everybody talks about baseball, but I really think football probably has a little bit more American feeling than anything.

Joe Montana

Yes, we've seen it all before. And yes, those who do not study history are condemned to repeat it. But no, the sky is not falling - baseball is such a great game that neither the owners nor the players can kill it. After some necessary carnage, market forces will prevail.

John Thorn

Your body is not made to throw like we throw. That's why you see softball pitchers pitching two or three games a day. It's a natural movement in softball. In baseball it's not a natural movement.

Jamie Moyer

My sports were team sports: ice hockey and baseball. The whole team dynamic is similar in business. Leadership is earned - the captain earns that role; it's not because he's the coach's son. These are all things we know, but in today's world, it's not a bad idea to remind ourselves.

James McNerney

Baseball presents a living heritage, a game poised between the powerful undertow of seasons past and the hope of next day, next week, next year.

John Thorn

You can't second-guess baseball. You can't second-guess yourself.

Mariano Rivera

I did a more serious turn in a movie called 'Moneyball.' It's a baseball movie, where I play the character of Scott Hatteberg, who was a professional baseball player for the Oakland A's in 2002. It was really intense. I lost almost 50 pounds in four months, learned how to hit the ball left-handed, and just immersed myself in the world of baseball.

Chris Pratt

My feeling is that when you're managing a baseball team, you have to pick the right people to play and then pray a lot.

Robin Roberts

God knows I gave my best in baseball at all times and no man on earth can truthfully judge me otherwise.

Shoeless Joe Jackson

For my children, they spent 15 to 20 years of their life in

baseball. And Ruth and I spent so many years of our married life that that was our life. We knew nothing else.

Nolan Ryan

Humanity is the keystone that holds nations and men together. When that collapses, the whole structure crumbles. This is as true of baseball teams as any other pursuit in life.

Connie Mack

I always dreamed of making it in baseball, but life has moved pretty quickly for me.

Mike Trout

Your job as a baseball player is to come to the park ready to play every day, and the manager, it's his job to make those decisions about who plays.

Cal Ripken, Jr.

We have an obligation to spread amateur baseball both at home and abroad. Building up the game at all levels - Little League, Babe Ruth Leagues, the colleges - is in our own self-interest. That's where the pool of talent is - and also of fans.

A. Bartlett Giamatti

Baseball was socially relevant, and so was my rebellion against it.

Curt Flood

Free agency screws everybody's allegiances up. Whether it be football, baseball, hockey, basketball, whatever it may be. It's really hard.

Bill Goldberg

When I was a freshman in high school, I got a letterman jacket, which you'd think would be great stock. The jacket had the big S on it, for Santa Monica. But rather than having a football or a baseball on the S, I had a little nine iron. Girls thought it was a flute.

Carson Daly

Up until the time I was 14 years old, I was sure that I was going to be a big-league baseball player. But that dream came to a rude awakening when I got cut from my high school baseball team.

Phil Knight

No matter what I talk about, I always get back to baseball.

Connie Mack

I love baseball - 'Moneyball' was my favorite book when I was 13.

Dylan O'Brien

I was playing little league baseball when Bruce Jenner was winning the gold but I don't think I was really paying attention at that time.

Dan O'Brien

My father - until the day that my dad died - didn't know how many points you scored in a touchdown. He could say there were nine innings in baseball, but no intricacies of the sport.

Damon Lindelof

When I was coming up, I just wanted to play baseball and I'm doing what I love to do most. How can I feel pressure doing what I love to do?

Miguel Cabrera

Hey, I'm just looking for an excuse to retire so I can play summer league baseball, go coach my nephews, play pickup basketball. I've always had that ability to move on to the next thing.

Doug Flutie

Baseball is this intense subculture that actually doesn't speak very much for the larger culture.

Michael Lewis

Whatever I contributed to the unique morale of the Cardinals was part of this growth, and so, of course, was my decision to have it out in public with the owners of organized baseball.

Curt Flood

People say, 'Weren't you deprived of your childhood?' No way. I would not take anything back at all. Everything about it was great. I got to go places, meet people, play baseball against older kids and better competition. I had a great time.

Bryce Harper

The trouble with baseball is that it is not played the year round.

Gaylord Perry

There are a lot of people who know me who can't understand for the life of them why I would got to work on something as unserious as baseball. If they only knew.

A. Bartlett Giamatti

I love baseball. And American Football, too. But not rugby.

Carlos Slim

Baseball would be a quite remarkable activity if it was the one place in the world where your co-workers didn't have any impact on how productive you were. But in fact, baseball is a high-stress occupation, and those sort of stress-inducing activities... just have a huge impact on how the team functions, I think.

Bill James

I wanted to definitely be a musician or a good preacher or a heck of a baseball player. I couldn't play ball too good - I hurt my finger, and I stopped that. I couldn't preach, and well, all I had left was getting into the music thing.

Muddy Waters

I like playing all sports, from football to soccer, and I love playing baseball.

Ryan Guzman

You have to have a lot of little boy in you to play baseball for a living.

Roy Campanella

Baseball is the life.

Steve Garvey

Back in my day, we didn't think about money as much. We enjoyed playing the game. We loved baseball. I didn't think about anybody else but the Cardinals.

Stan Musial

The great thing about baseball is the causality is easy to determine and it always falls on the shoulders of one person. So there is absolute responsibility. That's why baseball is psychologically the cruelest sport and why it really requires psychological resources to play baseball - because you have to learn to live with failure.

Michael Mandelbaum

There's nothing like Opening Day. There's nothing like the start of a new season. I started playing baseball when I was seven years old and quit playing when I was 40, so it's kind of in my blood.

George Brett

Building a baseball team is like building a house. You look for the best architects, the best builders - and then you let them do their jobs.

Pat Gillick

I wanted to go on the red carpet with a baseball cap, t-shirt, and jeans. And I still do. Because that's really who I am.

Missy Peregrym

Maintain 'baseball cards' and/or 'believability matrixes' for your people. Imagine if you had baseball cards that showed all the performance stats. You could see what they did well and poorly and call on the right people to play the right positions in a very transparent way.

Ray Dalio

I built a baseball field in the lower part of our property and I'm always working on that. I got a wheelbarrow, a pick and a shovel, and I started to build a baseball field during writers' strike. We have boys and girls come over and we have clinics in the spring. It's called The Strike because it's named for the writers' strike.

John C. McGinley

I'm married to football, baseball is my girlfriend.

Deion Sanders

I was a hyper kid, so I didn't want to play baseball and wait for the ball to come to me. I wanted to play a sport where I could go get the ball.

Shane Larkin

The great thing about baseball is there's a crisis every day.

Gabe Paul

I got scars on my face that tell some kind of story. I'm looking in the mirror, and I got one scar that's really two scars - half from a baseball bat and half from playing football in college. I'll tell you, though, after a while, your face gets so wrinkled up you can hardly see them.

Kris Kristofferson

Before I joined professional baseball, I started umpiring in San Diego, California. I worked 155 games in a five-month season. For three years in a row, I was working tripleheaders on Saturday and doubleheaders on Sunday.

Doug Harvey

You know, when I was a young boy I used to play baseball in my back yard or in the street with my brothers or the neighborhood kids. We used broken bats and plastic golf balls and played for hours and hours.

Robin Yount

And of course in America you've got American football and baseball and all those other ball games, soccer has become a little niche that the women have kind of filled.

Parminder Nagra

That's what I love about acting. There's never a set role. You can be a firefighter, you can be a baseball player, you can be whatever you want in the acting world. I think I've found my calling.

Ryan Guzman

The only real game - I think - in the world is baseball.

George Herman

I was a baseball player and a football player at Stanford, so

I didn't play a lot of golf in college. I really started playing a lot after I turned pro and I had some time in the off-season.

John Elway

Baseball needs more superstars.

Bryce Harper

I always wanted to be a major-league baseball player.

Bryce Harper

I don't want everybody to just see the baseball side of me.

Bryce Harper

Baseball is more than a game to me, it's a religion.

Bill Klem

You should have seen Willie Wells play shortstop: as good as Ozzie Smith and a better hitter. How I wish people could have seen Ray Dandridge play third base, as good as

Brooks Robinson and Craig Nettles and all of those. He was bowlegged; a train might go through there, but not a baseball.

Monte Irvin

I'm a guy who just wanted to see his name in the lineup everyday. To me, baseball was a passion to the point of obsession.

Brooks Robinson

I had a chance to play for the Cuban national team during the 2009 World Baseball Classic, but at the time I never thought about leaving Cuba.

Yoenis Cespedes

The sentimentality of baseball is very deeply rooted in the American baseball fan. It is the one sport that is transmitted from fathers to sons.

Michael Lewis

If you spend any time in Washington you'll find nerds. What happens is most of them sublimate their fixations with comics, or baseball cards, or 1960s British comedies to policy minutiae and political arcana. But, like Christians in ancient Rome, you can still spot them if you know the signals.

Jonah Goldberg

Yeah, I miss it. You don't just break off a friendship you've had with a sport, and with all those you've met all over the country. We've got some friends, some very close friends, and you just sit back and think how fortunate you were having a career like that. And, actually, there's nothing in the game of baseball that hasn't happened to me.

Lou Boudreau

I think everybody has something that takes them away or makes them happier. To some people it's baseball or sports or knitting or the movies.

Sutton Foster

When McGwire started the home run mania, attendance came back. The owners understood that the sudden spike in homers wasn't accidental. All baseball knew it. But baseball is run on money, and home runs meant money. Baseball turned a blind eye.

Gary Sheffield

To the people out there, baseball is a simple sport. But it is complex. It is never easy.

Dave Winfield

It's a weird scene. You win a few baseball games and all of a sudden you're surrounded by reporters and TV men with cameras asking you about Vietnam and race relations.

Vida Blue

Baseball is a game of race, creed, and color. The race is to first base. The creed is the rules of the game. The color? Well, the home team wears white uniforms, and the visiting team wears gray.

Joe Garagiola

I figured my wife was about to start law school. If that whole baseball pitching thing didn't work out, I had something to fall back on. I figure I'd put a ring on her finger. Turns out she was the smart one. Turns out she was the gold digger, not me.

Tim Hudson

Baseball gives a growing boy self poise and self reliance.

Al Spalding

Every time I sit with our general manager at a baseball game, and there's number-cruncher and statistician guy - I'm sitting around - they start talking about stuff, and I say, 'What's that? I've never heard of that one before.'

George Brett

I live for the Red Sox. I thoroughly enjoy them. For whatever reason, baseball has been a lot more fun for me in recent years. I loosely follow the Patriots and I root for them. I loosely follow the Celtics and then it gets to playoff time and I don't miss a game. Same with the Bruins. I'm not the diehard fan anymore.

Doug Flutie

There will never be another Mariano Rivera. He was a friend and a champion of a teammate. He really cared about the game of baseball, the way it was played, and whatever it took to win that night.

Jorge Posada

Say this for big league baseball - it is beyond any question the greatest conversation piece ever invented in America.

Bruce Catton

You can't get real happy or real depressed when you play baseball. Baseball is a great sport in that it offers a player a lot of opportunities for atonement.

Mike Piazza

Cape Cod baseball dates back to the time of the Civil War. A poster at the Hall of Fame in Cooperstown touts a round-trip train ride from Hyannis to Sandwich on July 4, 1885 - the occasion of the 14th annual baseball game between Sandwich and Barnstable.

Jane Leavy

I also developed an interest in sports, and played in informal games at a nearby school yard where the neighborhood children met to play touch football, baseball, basketball and occasionally, ice hockey.

Steven Chu

Our economics are not baseball's economics. Our game is not baseball's game. Our owners are not baseball's owners, with one or two exceptions. Our union is not baseball's union. What we do has to be crafted and suited to address hockey, to address the NHL, to address our 30 teams and our 700-plus players.

Gary Bettman

I keep telling myself, don't get cocky. Give your services to the press and the media, be nice to the kids, throw a baseball into the stands once in a while.

Vida Blue

I played football in high school, I played baseball when I was younger, things like that, but I think it was the passion I had for track where you want to do an individual sport and be the best, I think - there's nothing that can replace that.

Tyson Gay

If you could equate the amount of time and effort put in

mentally and physically into succeeding on the baseball field and measured it by the dirt on your uniform, mine would have been black.

Mike Schmidt

That was one of the most comfortable things about leaving baseball was to leave the environment. It's very much like a rock star existence - the nightlife, the hotels, lack of privacy... There's a lot of temptations out there. It was nice getting away from it.

Mike Schmidt

I had an extremely boring time doing 20 to 30 trades a day while everyone was talking about baseball or basketball. So I stood there fantasizing about a device that could do the same thing I was doing.

Thomas Peterffy

I love what I do. I'm appreciative and I'm still competitive. I still love baseball, but it doesn't consume me. If I can't do it anymore, then I go home and do something else. It's not the end of the world. It's just the end of your career.

Dontrelle Willis

Baseball is a game of averages, but over a short period of time, to have a little luck going is not a bad thing.

Bill Buckner

I was a baseball player. I played in high school and a little bit in college. I was a catcher. I don't know if I could have played any other position. As a catcher, you're always on the ball.

Tim DeKay

I think I understand why baseball players today are a little standoffish, because the world has changed. You don't know who's trying to take advantage of you, what people really want.

Billy Williams

For a quarter of a century, I've been playing baseball for pay. It has been pretty good pay, most of the time. The work has been hard, but what of it? It's been risky. I've broken both my legs. I've sprained everything I've got between my ankles and my disposition. I've dislocated my joints and fractured my pride.

Rabbit Maranville

Baseball grew rapidly in favor; the field was ripe. America needed a live outdoor sport, and this game exactly suited the national temperament. It required all the manly qualities of activity, endurance, pluck, and skill peculiar to cricket, and was immeasurably superior to that game in exciting features.

John Montgomery Ward

I belong to an improv group, I play cello, I have these phases - fencing, tae kwon do, baseball, ice hockey, boogie boarding in the summer, snowboarding in the winter.

Ty Simpkins

My eight years in Detroit, obviously, were my most successful years managing. I think that Pittsburgh and Detroit are probably very, very similar. We kinda rekindled the fire of baseball in Pittsburgh. We did the exact same thing in Detroit.

Jim Leyland

We lived near a playground that had four baseball

diamonds on it, and when I got to be 11, 12 years old, I was always over at the ballpark practicing or playing or doing something pertaining to baseball. And when I wasn't doing that, I was bouncing a rubber ball off the steps of my front porch at home.

Bobby Doerr

When I went to high school, my most passionate desire was to be a professional baseball player. But something within me told me that was not going to happen.

Tom Wolfe

People who write about spring training not being necessary have never tried to throw a baseball.

Sandy Koufax

I watch a lot of baseball on the radio.

Gerald R. Ford

Baseball has long been a national pastime that many Americans have cherished.

Jim Sensenbrenner

Baseball is about talent, hard work, and strategy. But at the deepest level, it's about love, integrity, and respect.

Pat Gillick

There are only five things you can do in baseball - run, throw, catch, hit and hit with power.

Leo Durocher

Those companies that don't see the black and brown communities are missing, out of their closed eye, talent, which leads to money and growth. When baseball, football and basketball couldn't see the field, they missed talent and growth. The same is true in the tech industry.

Jesse Jackson

I'll play baseball for the Army or fight for it, whatever they want me to do.

Mickey Mantle

I love baseball. I'll probably end up one of those old farts who go to spring training in Florida every year and drive from game to game all day.

Steve Earle

I started in the lowest league in baseball, and I worked my way all the way up to Triple A and then to the big leagues. I never reached the level that I thought I would reach as a player. But that's the way it goes. So then I started from the bottom as a manager, and I worked my way up to managing the Dodgers for 20 years.

Tommy Lasorda

I bet on the game of baseball and I bet on my team, even the mistakes I made, I have to take a different look at someone betting against their own team... that's throwing the game.

Pete Rose

Always wanted to be a Major League player. Loved baseball. Followed it. Loved to play. Plus, I could always hit.

Stan Musial

Baseball is dull only to dull minds.

Red Barber

Baseball is a game of inches.

Branch Rickey

Ethnic prejudice has no place in sports, and baseball must recognize that truth if it is to maintain stature as a national game.

Branch Rickey

Only in baseball can a team player be a pure individualist first and a team player second, within the rules and spirit of the game.

Branch Rickey

I'm not a great deductive thinker, but I will admit to having competence in a very wide range of things - not being afraid to try to write about baseball, choral music and dinosaurs in the same week and see connections among them.

Stephen Jay Gould

Almost all of us growing up have played baseball on some level. It has an inside track with people. It has a unifying effect.

Vin Scully

Baseball is a simple game. If you have good players and if you keep them in the right frame of mind then the manager is a success.

Sparky Anderson

Whoever wants to know the heart and mind of America had better learn baseball.

Jacques Barzun

What cracks me up is people who think I don't take baseball seriously. It's the most important thing in my life. They don't know how hard it is for me to get a bad game out of my mind. I still can't, but I'm getting better.

Brady Anderson

It's such a beautiful sport, with no politics involved, no

color, no class. Only as a youngster can you play and as a pro can you win. The game has kept me young, involved and excited and for me to be up here with gems of baseball.

Jack Buck

To give you an idea what it feels like to be going in with some of the best baseball players of all-time, I mean it is fantastic. I have to say this about them, there are so many of these guys up here that were my role models, people I looked up to, people I wanted to be like.

Dave Winfield

I think it puts baseball back on the map as a sport. It's America's pastime and just look at everyone coming out to the ballpark. It has been an exciting year.

Mark McGwire

Major League Baseball has always recognized the influence that our stars can have on the youth of America. As such, we are concerned that recent revelations and allegations of steroid use have been sending a terrible message to young people.

Bud Selig

Owners, the way they blackballed me from baseball, the way they used me, in a sense, and then the way they wanted to send a signal to the other players, saying, you know, we're going to get Jose Canseco out of the game. This is a cue or a message for you other guys to stop using steroids because the owners lost total control of the steroid use.

Jose Canseco

Cyclists, I work with a number of cyclists. They are great athletes; they are great aerobic athletes. If you ask them to hit a baseball or golf ball, they can't do that.

Eric Heiden

You know this baseball game of ours comes up from the youth. That means the boys. And after you've been a boy, and grow up to know how to play ball, then you come to the boys you see representing themselves today in our national pastime.

George Herman

Whether you want to or not, you do serve as a role model. People will always put more faith in baseball players than anyone else.

Brooks Robinson

I like contemporary American literature and I like biographies and I like jazz and I like baseball and I like writers who write about the human condition and sci-fi is just something that I happened into.

Jonathan Frakes

In baseball you hit your home run over the right-field fence, the left-field fence, the center-field fence. Nobody cares. In golf everything has got to be right over second base.

Ken Harrelson

Toledo is better than exciting, it's happy. Because nothing is more conducive to unhappiness than taking yourself seriously, and taking yourself seriously is difficult when you're baseball team is the Mud Hens.

P. J. O'Rourke

Taking in a baseball game on TV is also a big treat.

Jerry Seinfeld

There's different kinds of laughs. It's like a baseball lineup: this guy's your power hitter, this guy gets on base, this guy works out walks. If everybody does their job, we're gonna win.

Jerry Seinfeld

Most movies suck, even the independent ones. Hollywood is like baseball: Hit three good ones out of 10 and you're a Hall of Famer.

Denis Leary

Playing baseball for a living is like having a license to steal.

Pete Rose

I had an addiction to play baseball.

Pete Rose

Never bet on baseball.

Pete Rose

I love to be in the ballpark. I love to just go in and enjoy a great baseball game, a great pitchers' duel.

Magic Johnson

Baseball's Opening Day is full of time-honored traditions: the President throws out the first ball, the Cubs' starting pitcher walks away with a 54.00 ERA, the Royals get mathematically eliminated from the pennant race.

Rob Sheffield

My dreams do not end with playing Major League Baseball.

Derek Jeter

A lot of older parents worry about being older parents. I hear people say, 'I don't want to be too old to play baseball with my son.' They worry that their kids will be embarrassed by their parents' age.

Penn Jillette

Any one game in baseball doesn't tell you that much, just as any one poll doesn't tell you that much.

Nate Silver

It seems women are expected to be so much more than men, which means we have to work that much harder. We're the ones under the microscope. We're expected to sound perfect. We're expected to look perfect all the time. We're expected to be style-setters, whereas the boys roll onto the stage in their jeans, T-shirts and baseball caps.

Carrie Underwood

I'm no different than others with cancer. I just happen to play professional baseball. I'm part of those statistics that cancer has touched as well.

Eric Davis

A tall, thin old man waving a scorecard from the corner of his dugout. That's baseball.

Ernie Harwell

Baseball is the president tossing out the first ball of the season. And a scrubby schoolboy playing catch with his dad on a Mississippi farm.

Ernie Harwell

Baseball is played by all countries now, and softball, too.

Tommy Lasorda

You can have the best team in baseball, and if nobody goes through the turnstiles, you've got to shut the doors down.

Tommy Lasorda

Preschoolers have a way of grabbing your attention. Mine help me not to be a baseball player at home.

Dan Quisenberry

I was hitting .360 when I was diagnosed. I didn't forget how to play while I was recovering. I don't know if the cancer is gone for good. I don't think anyone ever knows, but no one is going to steal my joy for as along as I'm able to play baseball.

Eric Davis

Doctors tell me I have the body of a thirty year old. I know I have the brain of a fifteen year old. If you've got both, you can play baseball.

Pete Rose

I can't remember, I wish I could remember the first time I bet on baseball.

Pete Rose

I don't go to bed every night worried about getting back into baseball.

Pete Rose

I love the fans, I love the game of baseball, and I love Cincinnati baseball.

Pete Rose

Looking back on those days and little leaguer, the Hall of Fame is not even a blinking star, but through baseball travels and moving up the ladder, that star begins to flicker.

Wade Boggs

Baseball has better opening days and All-Star Games than the N.F.L. does. Ours stink.

John Madden

I don't know anything about baseball.

Sean Connery

So, baseball is probably more physical of the two mentally.

Bo Jackson

When I took the job as the manager of the Olympic team, I didn't take it because I was a Dodger. I did it because I was an American, and I wanted to bring that gold medal where it belongs in baseball, the United States. And that's exactly what our team did.

Tommy Lasorda

I'm a sports-watcher. I played football and baseball, coached baseball. So I watch those things.

Phil Jackson

There couldn't have been a better Hollywood ending for us. It's beyond baseball. It's rooting for your family.

Jimmy Fallon

Nicknames are baseball, names like Zeke and Pie and Kiki and Home Run and Cracker and Dizzy and Dazzy.

Ernie Harwell

The best example of how impossible it will be for Major League Baseball to crack down on steroids is the fact that baseball and the media are still talking about the problem as 'steroids.'

Malcolm Gladwell

Where would I be without baseball? Who am I without baseball?

Bob Uecker

Baseball has changed dramatically since I began my tenure with the Yankees.

Joe Torre

I was looking for something like baseball, where there's a lot of data and the competition was pretty low. That's when I discovered politics.

Nate Silver

Baseball wasn't easy for me.

Ryne Sandberg

I'd never heard of colon cancer. Baseball wasn't even important to me. I have a wife and two girls. That's what was important. The doctors told me and all I could say was, 'When are we going to get this thing out?'

Eric Davis

Baseball is a team sport played by individuals for themselves.

Joe Torre

In regards to steroids, I think we're all to blame, all of

baseball. I never realized how far-reaching this problem has been.

Joe Torre

Just as the common law derives from ancient precedents - judges' decisions - rather than statutes, baseball's codes are the game's distilled mores. Their unchanged purpose is to show respect for opponents and the game. In baseball, as in the remainder of life, the most important rules are unwritten. But not unenforced.

George Will

People wanna know how hard something is. How hard was that hit? How fast was that ball? How far did that home run go? I know that in baseball, people are always interested in that. And there's probably the same kind of interest in football, but we've never gotten to it. I'm not the technology guy that does it. But I tell someone we ought to do it.

John Madden

Trip Hawkins - and this was the early 1980s - was saying there's going to be a day when everyone has a computer and they're going to want to do more on it, including playing games. So he started up a company, EA Sports, and he was going to have three games, football, basketball and baseball. So I was the football game.

John Madden

Again, like I said, I went out to play the game of baseball because I love to play it. I did it right. I did it the right way. I worked hard doing it.

Roger Clemens

Traditionally, baseball punishes preening. In a society increasingly tolerant of exhibitionism, it is splendid when a hitter is knocked down because in his last at bat he lingered at the plate to admire his home run.

George Will

Defense to me is the key to playing baseball.

Willie Mays

Really, it's not harder to train for them because once baseball starts you play everyday almost.

Bo Jackson

I think that baseball games are like soap operas. If you watch five in a row, you know enough to get hooked.

Jennifer Garner

After Jackie Robinson the most important black in baseball history is Reggie Jackson, I really mean that.

Reggie Jackson

I am a hero worshiper. I love the number one tennis player. I love the number one baseball player. I want to see those records broken.

Martha Stewart

One strange quality of writing about political campaigns is that it's a little like writing about a baseball game inning by inning. We presume we can say something about the final result from the state of play a third of the way through. You can when a game is a colossal blowout, but you can't when it's close.

John Podhoretz

While I'm playing baseball, I'm still writing songs and

having tapes sent to me. I'm sure I'll spend a lot of time in the whirlpool resting these tired bones, so I'll be thinking of music then.

Garth Brooks

America brought us the baseball cap; it's one of my favorite hats.

Philip Treacy

Whoever wants to know the heart and mind of America had better learn baseball, the rules and realities of the game - and do it by watching first some high school or small-town teams.

Jacques Barzun

I don't know where the loyalty lies in baseball. You really don't have to protect each other much, unless there's like a bench-clearing brawl. In hockey, it's important that they look out for each other.

Seann William Scott

The money I saved during baseball was probably all gone.

I'm tapped out.

Curt Schilling

Imagine if baseball were taught the way science is taught in most inner-city schools. Schoolchildren would get lectures about the history of the World Series. High school students would occasionally reproduce famous plays of the past. Nobody would get in the game themselves until graduate school.

Alison Gopnik

And my father didn't have money for me to go to college. And at that particular time they didn't have black quarterbacks, and I don't think I could have made it in basketball, because I was only 5' 11". So I just picked baseball.

Willie Mays

For many in baseball September is a month of stark contrast with April, when everyone had dared to hope. If baseball is a lot like life, as pundits declare, it is because life is more about losing than winning.

John Thorn

Baseball player. Yeah, that was my dream before acting, or alongside acting.

Shemar Moore

I have been a fan all my life, but now I have been out of football for over 10 years, and out of baseball for a little over six years and I don't go to games.

Bo Jackson

I found out early in life that I could hit a baseball farther than most players, and that's what I tried to do.

Harmon Killebrew

Honestly, I'm on the road so much that I never really get a chance to go to baseball games.

Young Jeezy

When I was a kid, I was always an athlete. I played a lot of sports. I played football, basketball, baseball and soccer.

Scott Caan

And when I retired, trust me, not only did Nolan Ryan, but the entire Ryan family had withdrawals from baseball. And it was tough.

Nolan Ryan

I can honestly say it took two full years for me to get over the fact that I was no longer a baseball player.

Nolan Ryan

I was lucky enough to have the talent to play baseball. That's how I treated my career. I didn't think I was anybody special, anybody different.

Carl Yastrzemski

The Red Sox are the local scapegoats. It's hard enough to play baseball without being the local scapegoat too.

Michael Lewis

No player in baseball history worked harder, suffered more, or did it better than Andre Dawson. He's the best I've ever seen.

Ryne Sandberg

There's something magical about a home run. It almost violates the space of the stadium. It's a game of the imagination in some ways. Baseball.

Alex Gibney

Normally, some people think about 50 as a big moment in life. I kind of think 30 because in your baseball career, 30 was considered on top kind of looking at the end of your career. So I remember thinking about 30 in different ways, but 50 just seems like another step right now.

Cal Ripken, Jr.

Of all the plays in baseball, stealing home is by far the most exciting.

Cheech Marin

When you are away from the game and busy with other areas, you realize that the world does not revolve around baseball.

Cal Ripken, Jr.

Major League Baseball has prostate awareness for two weeks leading up to Father's Day, and I want to get involved in that.

Steve Garvey

The great thing about baseball is when you're done, you'll only tell your grandchildren the good things. If they ask me about 1989, I'll tell them I had amnesia.

Sparky Anderson

I mean the game is just, everybody talks about baseball but I really think football probably has a little bit more American feeling than anything.

Joe Montana

Baseball is a public trust. Players turn over, owners turn over and certain commissioners turn over. But baseball goes on.

Peter Ueberroth

Sitting at a candidate rally is similar to sitting in a ballyard.

Both give you the opportunity to assess the technical metrics and reflect on the intangibles - what baseball calls 'make up' and politics calls 'character' - the leadership, talent and maturity to add value to a venture.

Christine Pelosi

A baseball manager is a necessary evil.

Sparky Anderson

We're the best team in baseball, but not by much.

Sparky Anderson

On matters of race, on matters of decency, baseball should lead the way.

A. Bartlett Giamatti

That's one of the great oddities of baseball: Success is relative. A hitter who fails 70 percent of the time at the plate is a potential member of the National Baseball Hall of Fame, and many World Championship teams lose more than 70 games during their title-winning seasons.

Don Yaeger

Donning a glove for a backyard toss, or watching a ball game, or just reflecting upon our baseball days, we are players again, forever young.

John Thorn

Baseball is one of the most beautiful games. It is. It is a very Zen-like game.

Jim Jarmusch

I live in L.A., so I go to basketball games. But I love baseball.

Penny Marshall

New York is great, but the New England fans are probably the most knowledgeable and ardent fans, and not just in baseball, but all sports. But Red Sox Nation is Red Sox Nation.

Dick Williams

Like a lot of kids, you kind of think baseball's boring - that's the perception.

Tony Gwynn

Baseball may be our national pastime, but the age-old tradition of taking a swing at Congress is a sport with even deeper historical roots in the American experience. Since the founding of our country, citizens from Ben Franklin to David Letterman have made fun of their elected officials.

Evan Bayh

I have to play baseball to make me happy. I have to be an athlete. But when it's all said and done, I'll be a normal father. A normal-type house man.

Rickey Henderson

I keep a lot of my old baseball hats, and if you look in the hats I've had since I started pitching, you'll see 'Philippians 4:13' written on the brim. That's the Scripture that gets me through the day because sometimes you can't do it all by yourself. You can't do it on your own, so you lean on Him.

Scotty McCreery

Baseball regards us as sheep.

Curt Flood

There's a lot to be said for going to baseball games for a living.

Willie Geist

I love the game of baseball.

Nomar Garciaparra

I've been on 'Criminal Minds' twice! On the first show, a boy brought kids out to the woods and was beating them with a baseball bat, but I got away. Then they brought Tracy, my character, back - as a kidnapped girl. They saved me two times! Tracy lived!

Elle Fanning

The worst drivers are women in people carriers, men in white vans and anyone in a baseball cap. That's just about everyone.

Paul O'Grady

Do we need to have 280 brands of breakfast cereal? No, probably not. But we have them for a reason - because some people like them. It's the same with baseball statistics.

Bill James

We all used to collect baseball cards that came with bubble gum. You could never get the smell of gum off your cards, but you kept your Yankees cards pristine.

Penny Marshall

The good rising fastball is the best pitch in baseball.

Tom Seaver

Baseball represents family. It represents my childhood.

Alyssa Milano

We used to play baseball back in that field and keep an eye out for the bulls.

Jim Fowler

My baseball career was a long, long initiation into a single secret: At the heart of all things is love.

Sadaharu Oh

I'd walk through hell in a gasoline suit to play baseball.

Pete Rose

The thing I like about baseball is that it's one-on-one. You stand up there alone, and if you make a mistake, it's your mistake. If you hit a home run, it's your home run.

Hank Aaron

Baseball is ninety percent mental. The other half is physical.

Yogi Berra

I knew at a young age, whether I was playing baseball or hockey or lacrosse, that my teammates were counting on me, whether it be to strike the last batter out in a baseball game or score a big goal in a hockey game.

Wayne Gretzky

Cricket is basically baseball on valium.

Robin Williams

When I was a kid, I have two dreams. I want to be a baseball player. Hometown, Hiroshima, has a Japanese baseball franchise team called Hiroshima Carps. You know, and then I want to be a sushi chef. I want to make own restaurant - sushi restaurant.

Masaharu Morimoto

I see great things in baseball. It's our game - the American game.

Walt Whitman

In baseball, my theory is to strive for consistency, not to worry about the numbers. If you dwell on statistics you get shortsighted, if you aim for consistency, the numbers will be there at the end.

Tom Seaver

Growing up, I looked up to major league baseball players,

and now these young women have amazing, incredible women all across the board, from swimming to gymnastics to softball to basketball.

Jennie Finch

The obsessions of others are opaque to the unobsessed, and thus easy to mock. NASCAR, jazz, baseball, roses, poetry, quilts, fishing. If we're lucky, we all have at least one.

Roberta Smith

One night I went over to get some dope from some Hollywood tough guy. After I left, my son Scott, who was only fifteen, went over with a baseball bat to kill him. I was laughing out of one eye and crying out of the other. I thought, Who am I kidding?

James Caan

Baseball gives every American boy a chance to excel, not just to be as good as someone else but to be better than someone else. This is the nature of man and the name of the game.

Ted Williams

If people are a little nervous about approaching you at the market, it's good. I'm not Chuckles The Clown. Or Bozo. I don't cut the ribbon at the opening of markets. I don't stand next to the mayor. Hit your baseball into my yard, and you'll never see it again.

Tom Waits

Baseball happens to be a game of cumulative tension but football, basketball and hockey are played with hand grenades and machine guns.

John Leonard

I love sporting events and popcorn and pizza and being outside, like at a baseball or football game. I love amusement parks, going to ride roller coasters.

Carrie Underwood

If my uniform doesn't get dirty, I haven't done anything in the baseball game.

Rickey Henderson

The Statue of Liberty is no longer saying, 'Give me your

poor, your tired, your huddled masses.' She's got a baseball bat and yelling, 'You want a piece of me?'

Robin Williams

Baseball is a game where a curve is an optical illusion, a screwball can be a pitch or a person, stealing is legal and you can spit anywhere you like except in the umpire's eye or on the ball.

James Patrick Murray

You could be a kid for as long as you want when you play baseball.

Cal Ripken, Jr.

Baseball is a red-blooded sport for red-blooded men. It's no pink tea, and mollycoddles had better stay out. It's a struggle for supremacy, a survival of the fittest.

Ty Cobb

If you're going to play at all, you're out to win. Baseball, board games, playing Jeopardy, I hate to lose.

Derek Jeter

Baseball was made for kids, and grown-ups only screw it up.

Bob Lemon

Baseball is a game, yes. It is also a business. But what is most truly is is disguised combat. For all its gentility, its almost leisurely pace, baseball is violence under wraps.

Willie Mays

I could describe my career in two words: who knew. I was on the path to becoming a professional baseball player, but I got injured in college. When I decided to move out to L.A. to try acting, nobody was betting on me, not even my family. But it's always been that way for me; nothing has come easy.

Shemar Moore

I was born to play baseball.

Roberto Clemente

I could describe my career in two words: who knew. I was

on the path to becoming a professional baseball player, but I got injured in college. When I decided to move out to L.A. to try acting, nobody was betting on me, not even my family.

Shemar Moore

I'd love to stay in baseball, but I won't beg. I'd love to work with young umpires. I think I could teach them, help them develop. I can spot flaws, help them get over the hump. You're striving for perfection every game, yet you never achieve it. If baseball wants me, I'm available.

Doug Harvey

Baseball can be slow in many ways. The action starts with when the pitcher delivers the ball. But the action really starts when the crack of the bat happens.

Cal Ripken, Jr.

I kept thinking, 'this must be the coolest job - I'd like to be a professional baseball player.' They were getting paid to play a game, and what a cool lifestyle that was.

Cal Ripken, Jr.

My dream was to play football for the Oakland Raiders. But my mother thought I would get hurt playing football, so she chose baseball for me. I guess moms do know best.

Rickey Henderson

I love being an older comic now. It's like being an old soccer or an old baseball player. You're in the Hall of Fame and it's nice, but you're no longer that person in the limelight on the spot doing that thing.

Eric Idle

Some of my finest memories are from my time at the University of Texas. College baseball, I love it.

Roger Clemens

Baseball people, and that includes myself, are slow to change and accept new ideas. I remember that it took years to persuade them to put numbers on uniforms.

Branch Rickey

I've always been like that. I was a tomboy when I was a kid, so I was always playing baseball and basketball and football and stuff as a kid with the boys.

Catherine Bell

Before, if I wasn't in baseball, I wanted to become a doctor.

Pedro Martinez

I miss baseball.

Dale Murphy

Tipping your hat to a lady is good form. If you're at a dinner table, you'd most certainly take your hat off - cowboy hat, baseball hat, or otherwise.

Lyle Lovett

That's how easy baseball was for me. I'm not trying to brag or anything, but I had the knowledge before I became a professional baseball player to do all these things and know what each guy would hit.

Willie Mays

The greatest challenge I think is adjusting to not playing baseball. The reason for that is I had to come out of baseball and come into the business world, not being a college graduate, not being educated to come into the business world the way I should have.

Willie Mays

I don't know what you guys say, but at home, life is way different from baseball.

Barry Bonds

I was a momma's boy. I didn't get anything from Dad, except my body and baseball knowledge. The only time I spent with him was at the ballpark.

Barry Bonds

Young players need to know how to take care of themselves for life after baseball.

Barry Bonds

Casey knew his baseball. He only made it look like he was fooling around. He knew every move that was ever invented and some that we haven't even caught on to yet.

Sparky Anderson

Like baseball, food will never go out of style; we will always need to eat and we will always find it entertaining. I think of food TV this way - all the fun and none of the calories.

Gail Simmons

Baseball needs to put the steroids era behind it by having and enforcing tough rules against all kinds of artificial advantages, so that spring can return.

Marvin Olasky

If you're a singer you lose your voice. A baseball player loses his arm. A writer gets more knowledge, and if he's good, the older he gets, the better he writes.

Mickey Spillane

Baseball fans are collectively the '10th man' and needed most when team performance is shaky. When mistakes are made, there's no need to heckle your team - that's what the other side is for!

Christine Pelosi

Baseball loyalists cite the game's legendary numbers - 300 wins, 500 homers, 3,000 hits - as evidence of the sport's elegance, beauty, and gravitas. What no one mentions is how wretched and painful it is to actually watch a former star gasp and sputter his way toward a legendary number.

Stephen Rodrick

This is a great thing that's happening in baseball. We don't know if it will ever happen again.

Mark McGwire

Making the Hall of Fame, would it be something that's gratifying because of what I've sacrificed? Sure. Baseball has been a big part of our lives. We've sacrificed our bodies. It's the way we made our living.

Barry Bonds

When I was a kid, I played sports a lot. My mom and dad were divorced, but I hung out in the neighborhood a lot, and it was all about sports. I would be out all day on the sand lot or on the hockey rink. My dad would take me to baseball games, but he worked so hard, and he would always fall asleep.

Alex Gibney

I want to play music when I want, write a song if I want or watch a baseball game if I want.

John Lee Hooker

Baseball always gets credit for the foundational part of masculinity - the father thing. The eternal game of backyard catch, 'Field of Dreams', the Ripkens, the Griffeys, the Bondses, so on. But football is the real paternal game, because it's a conveyor belt of father figures, in the form of coaches.

J. R. Moehringer

Baseball is a red-blooded sport for red-blooded men. It's no pink tea, and mollycoddles had better stay out.

Ryan Cabrera

You kind of took it for granted around the Yankees that there was always going to be baseball in October.

Whitey Ford

In a tradition second in wonderful absurdity only to 60-year-old baseball managers wearing uniforms and spikes in the dugout, golf spectators come dressed ready to play 18.

Willie Geist

You look around baseball and when things go south, that type of fan apathy happens.

Mike Quade

American history and the history of baseball are bound up together: our racial politics can be described and traced through it.

Chad Harbach

There's certainly a large literature around baseball in the U.S.

Chad Harbach

Statistics are to baseball what a flaky crust is to Mom's apple pie.

Harry Reasoner

That's what Major League Baseball's steroid scandal was all about, the hidden harm in competitive sports that sends the wrong message to the young.

Suzanne Fields

My motive, and I will make it clear and look you in the eyes, is to attack major league baseball. That's my motive.

Jose Canseco

I didn't get a ton of interest from colleges in baseball and football, but I was outstanding in track and had the sense that this would be my meal ticket... Track was a sport where I saw immediate improvement, and I had a lot of good support behind me... and the coaches had a lot of experience and pushed me in that direction for sure.

Dan O'Brien

Hey, it's been a great ride for me, a great life. Everything I have I owe to baseball. Baseball owes me nothin'. Ain't nobody has to give me nothin'. I would be embarrassed if I had a day somewhere. I don't want no day. I want friends, to live my life the way I wanna live it.

Don Zimmer

I love the MLB app, because I'm a pretty obsessed baseball fan.

Bill de Blasio

Major League Baseball is a national institution and we take our responsibilities seriously when it comes to how the game affects the lives of American youth.

Bud Selig

And then came the nineties, when management, suddenly frightened that they had ceded control to the players, sought to restore baseball's profitability by 'running the game like a business.'

John Thorn

I just try to do what I have to do and let the people out there do what they have to do, which is have fun, scream, yell and jump around. I try to do what I have to do, which is play baseball, and I can only play in that piece of area there, so that's what I try to do.

Pedro Martinez

There are more people killed with baseball bats and hammers than are killed with guns.

Paul Broun

Hitting a baseball well, as in cricket, is a very rare skill. One of most difficult things to do in the world to do, hitting a ball coming at you at ninety miles an hour with a round bat. Wonderful to watch.

Peter Tork

Tennis was always there for me, which was lucky. I would go play baseball, basketball, football, hang with my brother, do whatever, and at the end of the day I'd come back and say, 'Hey, Mom, would you hit 15 minutes worth of balls with me?'

Jimmy Connors

When you're an expert in a subject, you can retain new factoids on your favorite topic easily. This only works for the subjects you're truly passionate about, though. Baseball fans can reel off stats for their favorite players, then space out on their own birthday.

Clive Thompson

I think some of the pressure comes from the expectations of other people. Like if your father played baseball, they expect you to be the big lifesaver or something when you play a sport.

Barry Bonds

I went through baseball as 'a player to be named later.'

Joe Garagiola

I was a baseball player at North Central High School in Spokane, Washington even though I was all-city in basketball, even when I signed a letter of intent to play quarterback at Washington State.

Ryne Sandberg

If I had any interest in coming back to baseball, it would be as a general manager and not as a manager.

Lou Brock

The baseball held was my fantasy of what life offered.

Lou Brock

The Atlanta Braves are really all that our children know about this crazy baseball life, and we are so thankful for this upbringing for them.

Tim Hudson

Willie Mays was the best baseball player I ever saw. He could do anything.

Doug Harvey

No game in the world is as tidy and dramatically neat as baseball, with cause and effect, crime and punishment, motive and result, so cleanly defined.

Paul Gallico

I've got a lot of years to live after baseball and I would like to live them with the complete use of my body.

Sandy Koufax

I hope I never do anything to hurt baseball.

Home Run Baker

The more that Japanese players go to the big leagues to play and succeed, the more that will serve to inspire young kids in Japan to want to become baseball players when they grow up.

Ichiro Suzuki

I've only read two books in my life: Baseball Sparkplug and Love Story.

George Brett

If you seriously aspire to be a manager in the big leagues, there is a baseball 'book' that one must learn. Alongside that book, you must practice Spanish. Of 25 players on each roster, sometimes there are between eight and 15 players who speak Spanish.

Tony La Russa

As we all know, Cooperstown is the home of baseball. One of the many duties of the home plate umpire is to make sure that the runner touches home. Well, if you're a true baseball fan, you need to visit Cooperstown. This is home.

Doug Harvey

Balls and strikes are the basic tenet to everything in baseball. From the perspective of hitting, pitching, offense and defense, it's all about the strike zone and how the battle is waged there between the pitcher and hitter.

Doug Harvey

I sang the National Anthem at Dodger Stadium - at a baseball game - which was crazy; there was, like, 60,000 people there, which is a huge deal in America - singing the National Anthem.

Adam DeVine

The real beauty of it - key to my life was playing key

chords on a banjo. For somebody else it may be a golf club that mom and dad put in their hands or a baseball or ballet lessons. Real gift to give to me and put it in writing.

Vince Gill

Babe Ruth made a baseball fan of me. I used to go to Yankee Stadium just to see him come to bat.

Effa Manley

I would say I was jock. I went to Sierra College. I was a big baseball player. Getting into the MLB was my dream - to become a left-handed pitcher for the Yankees. That's what I was hoping, but life kind of went the other way.

Ryan Guzman

That's the remarkable thing about baseball. The game has a way of having you scratch your head one minute and drive you crazy, and then the next, you're entertained beyond your wildest hopes. That's why it's the best game.

Johnny Bench

From the time I went into baseball, I have always been

handicapped by my hands, which are too small. I never saw the day yet when I was able to span an ordinary baseball.

Pud Galvin

I have been blessed to win a number of awards and be involved in numerous historical baseball moments over my 20-year career with the Los Angeles Dodgers and San Diego Padres.

Steve Garvey

We are fortunate and blessed to have a partner of Harvey Schiller's stature, who shares our vision for the future of the Dodgers, the city of Los Angeles and our great baseball fans throughout the world.

Steve Garvey

Involvement in my kids' sports teams is something I have made time for over the years. I've also been able to coach all three of them in baseball and basketball, something that has strengthened our bonds and given me indescribable joy. I wouldn't trade it for anything.

Thomas Perez

I never want to sit out. I want to play baseball games.

Matt Kemp

I am involved in minor league baseball. I go around the country speaking to troubled youths, trying to help them understand that whatever path they choose, they'll need to really pay attention to it.

Gerry Cooney

I love sports. I've played basketball, baseball, soccer, tennis, track and field growing up.

Michael B. Jordan

I enjoy baseball more than anything and would like to be involved with it forever, but the reality is your survival is determined by how well you compete, not by your fondness for the game.

Sadaharu Oh

Never drew a paycheck outside of baseball.

Don Zimmer

I was playing little league baseball when Bruce Jenner was winning the gold, but I don't think I was really paying attention at that time. It wasn't until 1980 - I think I was 12 years old - that I thought, 'Wow that's what I want to do. I want to be on the Olympic team.'

Dan O'Brien

The vast majority of people who watch baseball can properly call 95% of all plays that happen on the field. My job is to teach you how to call the other 5%.

Jim Evans

I will calmly wait for my induction to the Baseball Hall of Fame. Don't I have the numbers to be inducted?

Sammy Sosa

A baseball team is like a band. Because, conceptually, there are no heroes in baseball - there's just the team.

Cass McCombs

I kind of dress like a boy from the nineties. I like wearing baseball hats. I just like to be really comfortable.

Mae Whitman

I think we have our sports within our own culture that are huge with baseball, football, basketball, and hockey. Those are the sports in America that we grow up with and soccer isn't really there yet.

Claudio Reyna

What you have to remember is that baseball isn't a week or a month but a season - and a season is a long time.

Chuck Tanner

I'm not an athlete, I'm a baseball player.

John Kruk

The student body was huge at UT and you had to mature pretty quick, very quick actually. I enjoyed it and it helped me a lot in my life in general - not only in the classroom but on the baseball field as well.

Roger Clemens

These days baseball is different. You come to spring training, you get your legs ready, you arms loose, your agents ready, your lawyer lined up.

Dave Winfield

I like watching baseball on TV. I love watching all the sports.

Bradley Steven Perry

Perhaps the truest axiom in baseball is that the toughest thing to do is repeat.

Walt Alston

I play to represent God, something bigger than baseball.

Albert Pujols

I'd never even been to Wrigley Field. I never even enjoyed baseball that much, but I loved being there, the crowd was lovely, and they all sang with me!

Bea Arthur

Five days after the Tsarnaev brothers blew up Boston's most sacred event, and just 24 hours after one brother was killed and the other was caught, everyone decided that it was OK to play baseball at Fenway again. The game happened on a Saturday afternoon, preceded by an emotional ceremony and many prayers.

Bill Simmons

I am old enough to remember every Red Sox season since 1975. Baseball is long. Baseball takes forever. It's day in, day out, for six solid months - seven if you're lucky. Winning is always fun.

Bill Simmons

I played baseball, and that's pretty much it. Basketball came late, this was, basketball was the sport that I tried to master, I kind of mastered baseball, so basketball was one of those things where I wanted to master this game, so that's why I probably play it the way I do.

Eric Williams

I'm really into basketball, baseball, football and working out - but you'll never catch me in a public sauna.

Joey Lawrence

I heard that in the United States the level of baseball was the highest in the world. So it was only natural that I would want to go there, as a baseball player.

Ichiro Suzuki

If you put a baseball and other toys in front of a baby, he'll pick up a baseball in preference to the others.

Tris Speaker

I did 'Kidulthood' and 'Adulthood,' and that's what people wanted and expect me to always do. They want me to do 'hood films and be the guy swinging baseball bats and saying 'Yo Blood' and beating up others in the street.

Noel Clarke

Just because you're down to your last strike, you're not out yet. You can always do more. You'll always have more at-bats to take. That's true in baseball, in rescuing animals, and in life, generally.

Tony La Russa

As a kid I was fascinated with sports, and I loved sports more than anything else. The first books I read were about sports, like books about Baseball Joe, as one baseball hero was called.

Robert Jay Lifton

It's a funny business. I kind of compare it to baseball. I'm always looking for a home run.

Billy Mays

Basketball's eras are defined by teams - Celtics, Lakers, Bulls - and baseball's epochs are defined by players - Ruth, Robinson, Mantle - but with football, it's the sideline strategists, the nutty professors and top coated Lears.

J. R. Moehringer

In '83, we went over to Amsterdam. I just remember people saying, 'Baseball's just starting over here. They're learning how to play the game of baseball.'

Mark McGwire

Some men like to go in for polo, for example, and spend thousands of dollars on ponies. Some go nuts for paintings, and give half a million for a hunk of canvas in a fancy frame. But my passion is baseball.

Tom Yawkey

It's no secret what's going on in baseball. At least half the players are using steroids.

Ken Caminiti

Baseball is all about pitching, and we know we have to improve our pitching.

Tom Hicks

I don't do stuff to be a star. I do it because I feel it's important for kids, African American kids, to see an African American face that plays baseball.

Matt Kemp

In Hollywood, for me, it's all about the movie stars and the singers. Baseball players don't draw too much attention; we're low key. I'm good with faces and sometimes bad with names, but I'll walk up to somebody if I know who they are... show them some love.

Matt Kemp

Baseball is like cricket, and I grew up in a country where they had cricket. So I understand cricket, soccer and basketball. I played basketball at the club level and a little bit in college, so that's why I'm a basketball fanatic.

Patrick Soon-Shiong

I have an older son, Josh, and growing up, he just didn't care that much for baseball. And that was fine. But Chaddie, he always wanted to go to the ballpark. He just kind of took to it right away.

Bruce Sutter

When I played, I never needed the spotlight, nor did I want it. I simply wanted to play baseball and be respected by my teammates and the opposing players.

Bruce Sutter

There's always, I guess, a philosophy that if you come in,

you want to change all the parts, you want to change everything over. I've always tried to preach that consistency and continuity are very, very important. So if I know the baseball people, and I know they're competent and could do the job, I don't see any reason to replace them.

Pat Gillick

We fought like heck for every player and every advantage, but we knew we were part of something bigger than ourselves. To me, that is what baseball is all about. I hope it is always what baseball is all about.

Pat Gillick

Babe Ruth didn't become her father until 18 months after he married her mother, Claire, on April 17, 1929, Opening Day of the baseball season. Julia was 12 years old.

Jane Leavy

By the 1880s, baseball was entrenched in the Cape's sandy soil. Semipro teams, commonplace before World War I, were organized into the first Cape Cod League in 1923 - Orleans joined the four original teams five years later. By 1940, the league had foundered on financial shoals and disbanded.

Jane Leavy

In the spring of 1957, Mickey Mantle was the king of New York. He had the Triple Crown to prove it, having become only the 12th player in history to earn baseball's gaudiest jewel. In 1956, he had finally fulfilled the promise of his promise, batting .353, with 52 homers and 130 RBIs. Everybody loved Mickey.

Jane Leavy

I went to a Christian all-boys' college one time to pick up my buddies so we could go play baseball, and I just remember walking through the halls, and there's all these crucified Jesuses. It's scary.

Evan Goldberg

I'm the youngest of five kids, and I wanted attention. And in Santa Barbara, there was lots of theater going on, so for that area, it was a little bit like playing Little League baseball. There were dance classes, theater classes, and I just loved it.

Anthony Edwards

In baseball, you've got to keep working.

Danny Bautista

When I was a little boy, my dream was to play baseball and leave Cuba.

William Levy

I hated baseball. I really didn't like baseball at all until someone decided they were going to pay me... Every year I played in the big leagues, the day the season ended, I called my buddies in West Virginia and said, 'I'll be home tomorrow.'

John Kruk

The Oakland clubhouse is a wonderful place. A lot of these guys feel like rejects. They were rejects and they feel - they can tell you how baseball screwed up.

Michael Lewis

There are several insights at the heart of the A's system that I think are wonderful for baseball. One, that it's a team game. That no one player is going to make that much of a difference to your team, so for god's sake don't go blow a quarter of your budget on one guy.

Michael Lewis

Stealing home is one of the most sensational plays in baseball. If the run thus scored is the winning tally, the play is, of course, all the more thrilling. It is a play that requires a lot of quick thinking to bring about a successful completion. The chap who has slow moving feet and a slower moving brain had better never try to steal home.

Billy Evans

Why are baseball managers the only coaches who dress up like the players?

Jay Mohr

And I found out, the other part of it is that I found out and in my desire to life successfully, that baseball fit very well into my life. It's been a great teacher, trainer, mentor and you'll see what I mean in the next few minutes that I have to speak.

Dave Winfield

But I'll tell you this, it started with my mother. I have to give her. God bless her and rest her soul. I had a good foundation at home, so when I was able to go off and do these things in baseball there was always support.

Dave Winfield

As far as sleeping goes, you're up and ready to go at six in the morning. Spring training was always a combination of relaxing and working, and I missed that quite a bit. I missed being around the ball field. A baseball. A bat. The smell of the uniform, you might say. Talking baseball. Seeing opponents as well as the Cubs.

Lou Boudreau

Everything I learned about the game of baseball, I learned from my dad.

Roberto Alomar

When I was a little boy, I didn't know what the Hall of Fame was. I was just playing the game of baseball, and I wanted to be just like my dad.

Roberto Alomar

Ethnic life in the United States has become a sort of contest like baseball in which the blacks are always the Chicago Cubs.

Ishmael Reed

He means as much as Roberto Clemente does to Latin people. Thank God I had the opportunity to know him. I wish my kids had the opportunity to be around him, because that's how I want my kids to live their lives. I want them to be like Stan Musial. Not the baseball player. The person. That's the respect I have for that man.

Albert Pujols

I was showing early symptoms of becoming a professional baseball man. I was lying to the press.

Roger Kahn

When you sign your name on the dotted line, it's more than just playing baseball. You have a responsibility to make good decisions and show people how things are supposed to be done.

Tony Gwynn

There is but one game and that game is baseball.

John McGraw

I played baseball my entire life, up through college and everything, so working out and being physically active was always a huge part of my life. I'll spend at least a couple of hours in the gym a day.

Tyler Hoechlin

If you rush in and out of the clubhouse, you rush in and out of baseball.

Pee Wee Reese

The public wouldn't like the perfect umpire in every game. It would kill off baseball's greatest alibi - 'We was robbed.'

Billy Evans

I knew I wasn't a baseball writer. I was scared to death. I really was afraid to talk to players, and I didn't want to go into the press box because I thought I was faking it.

Roger Angell

I'm glad that I just played baseball, because I'm sure I had a much longer baseball career than I would've had a football career. I did miss football, but I didn't miss some of the injuries from football.

Barry Larkin

We in the Negro leagues felt like we were contributing something to baseball, too, when we were playing. We played with a round ball, and we played with a round bat. And we wore baseball uniforms, and we thought that we were making a contribution to baseball. We loved the game, and we liked to play it.

Buck Leonard

I just always wanted to be a baseball announcer. I'm a huge Mets fan, and I wanted to be the next Bob Murphy. As far as careers go, that was the first career that I really thought about. Well, before that, I wanted to be a Mello Yello truck driver.

Logan Marshall-Green

My first year in baseball, there were only one or two reporters. My second year, I got to the Triple-A playoffs, there were four or five. When I came up in 1984, I never saw so many people.

Dwight Gooden

Going back down to the minors is the toughest thing to handle in baseball.

Gaylord Perry

Toughest job in baseball is the general manager. Second toughest is the hitting coach.

Ken Harrelson

Baseball is a man maker.

Al Spalding

That's all baseball is, is numbers; it's run by numbers, averages, percentage and odds. Managers make their decisions based on the numbers.

Rollie Fingers

When I got out of baseball, I got all the way out. I might watch a World Series game or something.

Rollie Fingers

Baseball is meant to be a contemplative game. They play music to draw young people to the game. If young people can't come to the game without music, then they should stay home.

W. P. Kinsella

I'm going through a divorce now. This is the second one, and like baseball, I'm not gonna get three strikes. I've been living by myself for five years and I'm very comfortable. I can play my guitar when I want to.

Buddy Guy

Baseball was a dream I gathered more splinters than hits.

Frank Perdue

I wonder why there is a designated hitter in baseball after all these years? As an experiment, it seemed like a swell enough idea, but you would think the novelty would have worn off by now and everyone would get back to playing baseball.

Jay Mohr

I think one of the most difficult things for anyone who's played baseball is to accept the fact that maybe the players today are playing just as well as ever.

Ralph Kiner

I do something that I don't think anyone else does. I warm up before a game. Baseball and basketball players warm up, so why shouldn't the announcer warm up?

Chick Hearn

It's very simple. We are asking baseball to come clean and set the record straight. Either baseball officials seriously want to rid their sport of doping, or they want to brush the issue under the carpet. So far, we haven't seen much evidence of the former.

Richard Pound

I'm not devastated over a baseball game. If somebody came

to me and said, 'Your wife is terminally ill.' Or, if my kids and wife get on a plane and I got a call that said, 'Something happened with the plane,' that's devastating.

Tom Glavine

The baseball fights, you don't ever see the squaring off like you do in hockey, and in some instances, that's where baseball fights can be potentially more dangerous because you've got guys running all over the place and people throwing punches at you that you don't even see half the time.

Tom Glavine

Why is it there are so many nice guys interested in baseball? Not me, I was a real bastard when I played.

Burleigh Grimes

Despite the situation in Cuba, I had a chance to play on the national team; and compared to other baseball players and other people in Cuba, I had the opportunity to live at a level that was not very high class but in the middle.

Yoenis Cespedes

Upsetting the dope is a favorite pastime in baseball. Past performances count for but little in the national pastime. Reputations don't get you anywhere. A club is judged solely on results, and to get results, you must win ball games.

Billy Evans

Baseball is what we were, and football is what we have become.

Mary McGrory

I started collecting baseball cards and basketball cards when I was younger. I have a CD collection that turned into a DVD collection, and I have a Jordan shoe collection. And I don't drink, but I have a wine collection. I just started a sweatshirt collection. Every city that I'm in, I buy a sweatshirt. It's just something that I do.

Marques Houston

I'm not as anti-sports as I've led people to believe - I've been to a Giants game. I've been to Giants Stadium and I've watched games. I've watched lots of them, you know? I don't really pretend to know what's going on, but I've been immersed in the excitement of watching sports, particularly football. I like baseball, probably more than football.

Kevin Corrigan

There is nothing like Ruth ever existed in this game of baseball. I remember we were playing the White Sox in Boston in 1919, and he hit a home run off Lefty Williams over the left-field fence in the ninth inning and won the game. It was majestic. It soared.

Waite Hoyt

When I came into baseball, I had one goal for my career - the Hall of Fame.

Justin Verlander

I've had a good time here in baseball. I love baseball. That's why I'm still around.

Red Schoendienst

There's nothing to it. Baseball isn't that tough to play.

Red Schoendienst

When I was real young I wanted to play baseball. I really

loved playing center field, but that was never anything I was really ever that good at. I played up until I was in ninth grade.

Ryan Sypek

Everyone thinks I'm this jock of a woman, but I didn't play any sports. I didn't even let my kids play baseball because I was afraid they were going to get hit by balls.

Patti Hansen

I kind of write about visual art the way Roger Angell writes about baseball, which is to say, you're writing about life: it's a somewhat focused, limited terrain in which you write about everything.

Lawrence Weschler

Baseball is not a lot of statistics to me. It's blood and tears.

Laraine Day

Let someone else be the world's greatest actress. I'll be the world's greatest baseball fan.

Laraine Day

My life as Mrs. Leo Durocher and baseball come first.

Laraine Day

In baseball, you can hit 40 home runs on a single-A-league team and never get paid a thing. But in a hedge fund, you get paid on your batting average. So you go to the worst league you can find, where there's the least competition.

Julian Robertson

I'm flattered that so many baseball people think I'm a Hall of Famer. But what's hard to believe is how one-hundred and fifty plus people have changed their minds about me since I became eligible, because I haven't had a base hit since then.

Richie Ashburn

I know better than anyone else that my time is near. I've had a good life, and you don't stop and complain at this stage of the game. I've made some mistakes, and I'd like to stay around a little longer and overcome them, but there isn't time. I'll miss baseball. That I know.

Joe Tinker

I liked baseball and sports and Garbage Pail Kids and comic books. I know what it's like to really adore something.

Todd Lowe

I think video games are a huge part of our society now. Having kids play baseball video games helps them understand and love the game. It could actually push them to get out there and play the game for real. That's great for the sport.

Justin Verlander

I'm made in the Dominican. I'm from baseball country.

Robinson Cano

I grew up in Westlake Villiage, a suburb of L.A. There was a guy there who was a fighter and was like, 'I'll teach you to box.' I started a little bit of boxing, then it crossed over into jiu-jitsu. I was into it for a little while, but then I started doing basketball, baseball, team sports.

Jonathan Lipnicki

As a kid, I grew up on a farm in Florida, and I did what most little kids do. I played a little baseball, did a few other things like that, but I always had the sense of being an outsider, and it wasn't until I saw pictures in the magazines that a couple other guys skate, I thought, 'Wow, that's for me,' you know?

Rodney Mullen

There are many kids in and out of baseball who think that just because they have some natural talent, they have the world by the tail.

Hack Wilson

I used to go to the comic store all the time. I was into comic cards, which are essentially baseball cards for comic book heroes. They have these cool stats on the back. I had collections of these things. I still have a lot of my collection at home.

Brett Dalton

Day baseball is now dead for all practical purposes. Sooner or later, the game will be played in its entirety at night, and as I've said before, then baseball will be squarely in the amusement, the entertainment business along with wrestling, midget auto racing and the trotting tracks.

Larry MacPhail

I don't really pretend to know what's going on, but I've been immersed in the excitement of watching sports, particularly football. I like baseball, probably more than football.

Kevin Corrigan

I didn't really grow up a comic book fanatic. I was a big baseball player, and my passion in life, in third grade, was collecting baseball cards. That was my childhood thing.

Alan Ritchson

That's what's great about baseball: some people are exceptional at the game, but still, even people that aren't very athletic, like me - I played Little League! It's one of those games in sports where even if you're not the greatest, you can still play.

Tom Guiry

Dad played with me a great deal, as dads should do, and

our chief sport was baseball. He bought me a hardball when I was three years old, and he used to sit in a rocker on the front porch while I sat on the grass in the yard, and we'd play catch by the hour.

Mordecai Brown

My father loved baseball and he cultivated my talent. I don't think he ever had any doubt in his mind that I would play professional baseball someday.

Bob Feller

I just love putting on the uniform; it's what I have done since I was 6 or 7 years old. It's the life I know. If I didn't love the life of baseball, I wouldn't work out like I do every winter.

Steve Finley

If the human body recognized agony and frustration, people would never run marathons, have babies, or play baseball.

Carlton Fisk

I have goals and ambitions, and I see myself as a lifelong

baseball student. I have certain philosophies that I'd like to test at some point at the big league level. The job of manager appeals to me, a coach appeals to me, at a different time frame.

Cal Ripken, Jr.

I could've played basketball, but my mind was on baseball. I didn't know what I was in for. In high school it was a matter of talent. No one told you what to do.

Eric Davis

Nowadays, they have more trouble packing hair dryers than baseball equipment.

Bob Feller

In baseball, I was a pitcher, which I hated because there was no action there.

Bo Jackson

Words can be like baseball bats when used maliciously.

Sydney Madwed

I don't like American football. I think it's boring and ridiculous and predictable. But baseball is very beautiful. It's played on a diamond.

Jim Jarmusch

I am dead set against free agency. It can ruin baseball.

George Steinbrenner

I was doing what I love to do: play baseball. Not going to complain about that.

Willie McCovey

And I'd be lying if I told you that as a black man in baseball I hadn't gone through worse times than my teammates.

Curt Flood

I'm always flattered when someone thinks of me as a potential commissioner of baseball.

Cal Ripken, Jr.

I think it's a natural fit, major league baseball and country music.

Joe Nichols

Despite reforms in steroid control, serious problems still occur in and out of baseball.

Jim Sensenbrenner

If you don't like the way the Atlanta Braves are playing then you don't like baseball.

Chuck Tanner

Baseball does become slow sometimes. It's totally unnecessary. The - you can play baseball fast. You can play it slow, and for some reason, we have chosen to play it slow, you know, which is unfortunate, but nothing you can do about.

Bill James

I'll play out the string and leave baseball without a tear. A man can't play games his whole life.

Brooks Robinson

I was a professional athlete, the best baseball player in the world at one point.

Jose Canseco

There's a lot of things more than baseball that I want to do.

Mariano Rivera

Every day I went to the ballpark in Yankee Stadium as well as on the road people were on my back. The last six years in the American League were mental hell for me. I was drained of all my desire to play baseball.

Roger Maris

A cloud hangs over baseball. It's a cloud called drugs and it's permeated our game.

Peter Ueberroth

They say baseball is a slow game. It sure doesn't seem that way when you're in the dugout. You think you have it figured out, but things come up quick.

Mike Quade

When you see Major League Baseball putting academies in other countries, obviously that throws up a red flag. You wonder why they ain't going up in our neighborhood. Bottom line, what I see, I talk about... I see it over and over. If anybody can show me I'm wrong, then show me.

Gary Sheffield

The reason I didn't take the baseball route is because they don't have rankings for baseball players.

Jim Courier

It's not in baseball's interest or the players' interest to be taking this stance. It's the people's game.

Fay Vincent

There are a lot of people who influenced me, nurtured me, helped me along the way. But I can just recall looking back, the first time I got my baseball glove. Put it on the wrong hand, all those kind of things.

Dave Winfield

What I miss when I'm away is the pride in baseball. Especially the pride of being on a team that wins.

Billy Martin

I wasn't athletic. I played baseball, but I was terrible.

Matt Long

People like us are afraid to leave ball. What else is there to do? When baseball has been your whole life, you can't think about a future without it, so you hang on as long as you can.

Willie Stargell

Baseball skills schizophrenically encompass a pitcher's, a batter's and a fielder's.

John Updike

My little brothers loved baseball. I'm not as big on that as basketball or football, but I understand the game.

Jurnee Smollett

When I'm traveling on tour, one of my favorite things to do is to throw a baseball cap on and go to a Target. The company has always been good to me. They've got such a great creative team.

Christina Aguilera

I wanted to play baseball!

Kareem Abdul-Jabbar

I was a baseball fan myself, I wanted to play baseball.

Kareem Abdul-Jabbar

No former player has owned a team in baseball.

Derek Jeter

Humbled by the fact that never in a million years would I ever thought that I would be on the same stage with all these great Hall of Famers and enshrined to the National Baseball Hall of Fame.

Wade Boggs

Baseball is a rookie, his experience no bigger than the lump in his throat as he begins fulfillment of his dream.

Ernie Harwell

I don't think baseball owes colored people anything. I don't think colored people owe baseball anything, either.

Bob Feller

I had a client who was a professional baseball player once, and he would go to clubs and dance for seven, eight, nine hours at a time. He wouldn't drink, he wouldn't take drugs - he just danced because he had so much physical energy; he was this amazing athlete.

Martha Beck

Baseball is not what I love. It's my job.

Eric Davis

I've been playing baseball since I was 5 or 6 years old. I've been on a schedule, pretty much, since I was in eighth, ninth grade. I look forward to not doing that.

Derek Jeter

I bet on baseball in 1987 and 1988.

Pete Rose

You know, baseball's not stupid. Baseball does what the fans want, usually.

Pete Rose

I was a very good baseball player and football player as a kid.

John Malkovich

Even if my father wasn't speaking to me, he would never, ever miss a baseball game.

Ryan Reynolds

I always get very calm with baseball.

Paul Simon

I always liked the defensive part of baseball.

Pete Rose

I never picked up my phone and called a bookmaker and bet on a baseball game from the clubhouse. Never.

Pete Rose

If baseball wants to get you, they've got enough resources and enough investigators that they'll find a way to get you.

Pete Rose

Since 1869, baseball has been doing pretty well.

Pete Rose

They haven't given too many gamblers a second chances in the world of baseball.

Pete Rose

I listen to NPR and baseball games when I'm in my car. I mean, exclusively NPR and baseball games, and that's it, as far as the radio.

Juliana Hatfield

I was late to the Knicks. My dad was a big fan. But I first started watching baseball; I became a Red Sox fan. My dad was a Mets fan. I wanted to have my own team and league.

Noah Baumbach

My real-life athletic career was not very much. I played Little League baseball.

Dennis Quaid

When you go to watch a baseball game, when you go to watch an NBA game, when you watch an NFL game, when you go to watch movies, the offering that those arenas are doing foodwise is 'all the hot dogs you can eat'; all the French fries you can eat; for $20 you can eat 20 hot dogs.

Jose Andres Puerta

It isn't me that people love. It's baseball.

Ernie Harwell

I was a very good baseball and football player, but my father always told me I was much more interested in how I looked playing baseball or football than in actually playing. There's great truth in that.

John Malkovich

I was acting when I was playing baseball.

Bob Uecker

Baseball has always been filled with negative statistics.

Joe Torre

I'd like to think a baseball picture is somewhere in my future.

Garth Brooks

Of course, I believe that Mike Piazza is probably the

greatest offensive catcher in the history of baseball, only got over 50%. Johnny Bench is the best catcher in the history of baseball, but Piazza has all the record for catchers as far as offensively.

Pete Rose

I was not good at team sports, I have to say. I'm quite good at individual sports, but I was not good at team sports, so I wasn't good at baseball and football.

Tom Ford

Once upon a time, growing up male gave little boys a sense of certainty about the natural order of things. We had short hair, wore pants, and played baseball. Girls had long hair, wore skirts, and, no matter how hard they tried, always threw a baseball just like a girl.

Kenneth R. Miller

Awards mean a lot, but they don't say it all. The people in baseball mean more to me than statistics.

Ernie Banks

I grew up playing hockey and baseball, so I wish I had time to get back into it, but living in L.A. and North Carolina, you have to take advantage of the golf. You find yourself at charity golf events or going to the Emmys and meeting Kevin Costner. You don't get to do as much fishing or hockey as you used to, but there are certainly other payoffs.

Diego Klattenhoff

Baseball is 90 percent mental and the other half is physical.

Yogi Berra

Major League Baseball has the best idea of all. Three years before they'll take a kid out of college, then they have a minor league system that they put the kids in. I'm sure that if the NBA followed the same thing, there would be a lot of kids in a minor league system that still were not good enough to play in the major NBA.

Bobby Knight

When baseball is no longer fun, it's no longer a game.

Joe DiMaggio

The best thing about baseball is there's no homework.

Dan Quisenberry

A baseball swing is a very finely tuned instrument. It is repetition, and more repetition, then a little more after that.

Reggie Jackson

Athletes and musicians make astronomical amounts of money. People get paid $100 million to throw a baseball! Shouldn't we all take less and pass some of that money onto others? Think about firefighters, teachers and policemen. We should celebrate people that are intellectually smart and trying to make this world a better place.

Kid Rock

Major league baseball has asked its players to stop tossing baseballs into the stands during games, because they say fans fight over them and they get hurt. In fact, the Florida Marlins said that's why they never hit any home runs. It's a safety issue.

Jay Leno

The only change is that baseball has turned Paige from a second class citizen to a second class immortal.

Satchel Paige

If I didn't make it in baseball, I won't have made it workin'. I didn't like to work.

Yogi Berra

Baseball players are smarter than football players. How often do you see a baseball team penalized for too many men on the field?

Jim Bouton

I never gave up as a player, and I won't give up as someone who wants to go to the Hall of Fame, because it's the ultimate goal for a baseball player or a football player or a basketball player.

Pete Rose

The crack of the bat, the sound of baseballs thumping into gloves, the infield chatter are like birdsong to the baseball starved.

W. P. Kinsella

I really love the togetherness in baseball. That's a real true love.

Billy Martin

I was all-state in four sports in New Jersey, but sometimes I couldn't get served at a restaurant two blocks from my high school. There were no job opportunities then... the only thing a black youth could aspire to be was a bellboy or a pullman or an elevator operator, or, maybe, a teacher. There was a time when all we had was black baseball.

Monte Irvin

I was born to hit a baseball. I can hit a baseball.

Barry Bonds

No one intuitively understands quantum mechanics because all of our experience involves a world of classical phenomena where, for example, a baseball thrown from pitcher to catcher seems to take just one path, the one described by Newton's laws of motion. Yet at a microscopic level, the universe behaves quite differently.

Lawrence M. Krauss

Baseball is like church. Many attend few understand.

Leo Durocher

I also tell them that your education can take you way farther than a football, baseball, track, or basketball will - that's just the bottom line.

Bo Jackson

I've got five grandkids. They play baseball, they play football, they play basketball. I go to all the games. You always have that urge to say something when you're watching them. But I've learned to keep it to myself. I've blurted out some things and embarrassed myself.

John Madden

In life, so many things are taken for granted, but one thing I can honestly say is that I took every day, enjoyed the game of putting on that uniform and playing the great game of baseball.

Wade Boggs

I was a baseball player, I taught baseball, and all of a sudden I was in the business world. Now I used the baseball world to talk about their product. Not too much, just enough to keep going. Just be yourself and you'll never have a problem. That's what I did.

Willie Mays

I owe baseball. Baseball don't owe me a damn thing.

Pete Rose

I always wanted to do a baseball book; I love baseball. The problem is that a very large part of my following is in non-baseball playing countries.

Bill Bryson

I've been wanting to do a book about baseball for the longest time, and nobody will let me do it. It's the one thing from America I really miss.

Bill Bryson

Believe it or not, I worked four summers in college as a

sports writer covering baseball for a parks and rec department in Bayonne, N.J.

George R. R. Martin

Playing baseball was my dream, and no amount of money could sway my opinion.

Willie Stargell

After getting out of the service and going into baseball I never wanted to do anything else.

Bob Uecker

No one ever asked what was my relationship with Bart Giamatti. We used to talk about baseball a lot as a player and a commissioner, just talk about the game, what could we do to help the game, where's the game going, he was pretty good.

Pete Rose

I always played sports when I was young. I played football and baseball for eight years. I loved football.

Taylor Lautner

Baseball, while you're doing it, you think it's going to last forever.

Joe Torre

In baseball, you're always moving people around.

Joe Torre

Major league baseball is about the history of the game. Baseball history is so important. It's so much more than money.

Joe Torre

I'm a baseball freak.

Dee Dee Myers

Also I'm a part of the people that I've worked with in baseball that have been so great to me, Mr. Earl Mann of Atlanta, who gave me my first baseball broadcasting job.

Ernie Harwell

If I walked back into the booth in the year 2025, I don't think it would have changed much. I think baseball would be played and managed pretty much the same as it is today. It's a great survivor.

Ernie Harwell

Baseball is a universe as large as life itself, and therefore all things in life, whether good or bad, whether tragic or comic, fall within its domain.

Paul Auster

One-third of all professional baseball players come from Latin America, and Sosa is following role models such as the late Roberto Clemente, a Puerto Rican, from whom he adopted the No. 21. Now he is a model for others.

Bill Dedman

My first job after my retirement from baseball was as a narrator for the Eastman Philharmonica.

Willie Stargell

So you have to be more mentally focused in baseball.

Bo Jackson

Honestly, I'm not a big fan of baseball.

Novak Djokovic

In baseball you have terrific data and you can be a lot more creative with it.

Nate Silver

I don't think there's any player that's more talented than Alex Rodriguez. He cares very deeply about doing well. Baseball is his life. He puts a lot of pressure on himself.

Joe Torre

I love my baseball, and I love my Phillies.

Chad Hurley

I have lots of favorites movies. I say this only because it's a favorite movie because it's a sport I love. I'm a huge baseball fan. There are movies I like as much as this, but I sort of single this movie out because I'm a baseball nut, and that's 'Field of Dreams.'

Rick Santorum

I haven't had the time to say, 'I'm retiring.' But baseball says, 'You're retired.'

Rickey Henderson

I've been able to do what I love and what I'm passionate about my entire life. I made, you know, an insane amount of money playing baseball.

Curt Schilling

I've got a wife, four kids, a business, and a baseball career.

Curt Schilling

Baseball has been good to me since I quit trying to play it.

Whitey Herzog

I wasn't really serious about acting - I was serious about baseball.

Kurt Russell

There's nothing bad that accrues from baseball.

A. Bartlett Giamatti

I was set to go to Oregon to play college baseball and football.

Harmon Killebrew

I don't play fantasy baseball anymore now because it's too much work, and I feel like I have to hold myself up to such a high standard. I'm pretty serious about my fantasy football, though.

Nate Silver

It's not like learning how to hit a curve ball in baseball.

Floyd Abrams

I think that to fully appreciate baseball, it helps to have been born in the U.S.

Khaled Hosseini

I had an opportunity to play baseball in college, but I just didn't want to go to school. I started focusing on my music and it was game over!

Jason Aldean

Kids who I grew up with, who I played ball with, basketball, baseball, and went to parties with - for whatever reason - they ended up in a fundamentally different place than I did. I'm the attorney general of the United States and they are ex-felons.

Eric Holder

One of the walls of my bedroom was a collage of about 15 years of baseball photos. I would cut out the baseball pictures from every issue and I had this huge montage of thousands of pictures.

Curt Schilling

I did make a choice when I got away from baseball to be there to get my kids off to college.

Cal Ripken, Jr.

Well, my favorite sport as a kid was clearly baseball.

Leigh Steinberg

In baseball, you pack your uniform in the clubhouse after a ball game, and you see it hanging up in your locker when you get to your next city.

Harmon Killebrew

But baseball bounced back in the next decade to reclaim its place as the national pastime: new heroes, spirited competition, and booming prosperity gave birth to dreams of expansion, both within the major leagues and around the world.

John Thorn

Baseball has undergone and absorbed a whole set of dislocations.

A. Bartlett Giamatti

Even though I play a professional sport now, I love college baseball.

Roger Clemens

How do you combat a man with a firearm? You don't combat him with a golf club, baseball bat or a knife. You combat him with another firearm.

Luke Scott

Finally, for all of us but a lucky few, the dream of playing big-time baseball is relinquished so we can get on with grown-up things.

John Thorn

I'm forever a Pittsburgh Pirates fan. Apparently I've picked the worst baseball team in the world.

Alex Pettyfer

In baseball you train the whole body, except for the hip and eyes.

Rickey Henderson

When I joined a baseball club, the boys of my own age, and a little older, played in the first nine, those younger than myself played in the second, and those still younger in the third, and I played with them.

Heber J. Grant

I've never had to pitch a movie to a studio. I usually just let people read the script, then I cast it. I always think pitching is for baseball.

Harmony Korine

I know it's tough. Everybody in baseball knows its tough. I'm just going to give it my best shot.

Mark McGwire

It was so difficult for the fans to understand my problems with baseball.

Curt Flood

My main lucky number is 9. That was my baseball number in high school. My other lucky number is 3, because that's the one I wore before I got to high school and had to pick a different one.

Jason Aldean

I grew up playing football and baseball.

Amar'e Stoudemire

I probably follow all sports a little bit. I like hockey quite a bit. I like football. I like college basketball when it gets down to March Madness. I like baseball. I enjoy them all. I watch them all.

Vince Vaughn

Even though my dad was a manager in the minor leagues, I still traveled around with him and saw it from the field out. Now, as an owner, you're kind of looking from the whole baseball activity from outside in, from a fan's perspective.

Cal Ripken, Jr.

I grew up in the '60s, which was a creative time, so it wasn't that big of a stretch to go from a baseball bat to a guitar to a film camera.

Abel Ferrara

Baseball gets better for whatever reason.

Rafael Palmeiro

I love baseball, and the door remains open.

Rafael Palmeiro

The fundamentals of baseball haven't changed, but how we can teach those fundamentals has. With an e-book, learning can be more rewarding and fun.

Dusty Baker

In over 160 years of recorded baseball history, no team had ever won a championship this way.

John Thorn

I am the best in baseball.

Reggie Jackson

Individual statistics, plate time and everything tend to come, but the most enjoyment I get out of baseball is actually winning.

Chili Davis

I understand business and understand the ugly face of baseball, which is the business part of baseball.

Pedro Martinez

You know one little way in which baseball changes us? We don't even think twice about Japanese names anymore. You know what I mean?

Bill James

That was real baseball. We weren't playing for money. They gave us Mickey Mouse watches that ran backwards.

Bill Lee

Back in East St. Louis, tennis wasn't the real thing. If you weren't playing baseball, basketball, football, you were kind of on the outside.

Jimmy Connors

Baseball is just my job.

Barry Bonds

When I finish playing, I think I'd like to coach college baseball.

Barry Bonds

If you're an American reader, you can love short stories the way other Americans love baseball; this is our game, people! We have more than two hundred years of know-how and knack, of creativity.

Amy Bloom

I grew up in New York City, where we played highly unorganized sports: stick ball, stoop ball, and the occasional game of baseball with no adult supervision.

Jeff Greenfield

I've always been a great lover of baseball.

Peter Lynch

I grew up with baseball; I played in Little League and went to games with my dad. But I, as I grew up, became more of a basketball fanatic than a baseball one.

Jonah Hill

I am amused by cricket because it seems to take longer than baseball and I like that. It seems like a sport I could have made up it - it takes several days to play and everyone wears sweaters. I can't confess to knowing what's going on at all.

John Hodgman

If you watch the history of baseball, teams come back, and sometimes they could have come back, but they give in or give up.

Tony La Russa

It's a sensitive thing, playing major league baseball.

Tony La Russa

I would change policy, bring back natural grass and nickel beer. Baseball is the belly-button of our society. Straighten out baseball, and you straighten out the rest of the world.

Bill Lee

Would I like to see baseball happen in Charlotte? Absolutely.

Anthony Foxx

If newspapers were a baseball team, they would be the Mets - without the hope for those folks at the very pinnacle of the financial food chain - who average nearly $24 million a year in income - 'next year.'

Eric Alterman

The only reason baseball's numerical touchstones have any significance is that most players - even the game's greats - peter out just barely before they reach them.

Stephen Rodrick

I think baseball - the baseball genre - is this mitt, to use a double pun there, to catch a whole bunch of themes.

Rachel Griffiths

It was a terrible day for baseball, it was a worse day for Congress.

Fay Vincent

I lived the baseball life as a kid, with my dad in it. And I lived the baseball life as an adult, because I was in it. When I retired, I wanted the opportunity to be a little bit more flexible and home-based for my kids.

Cal Ripken, Jr.

I stayed attached to baseball through the kids and through minor league baseball, and I'm very satisfied with the schedule it allows me to have, which means I'm home until my kids go off to college. I value that time.

Cal Ripken, Jr.

Sadly, this problem of steroid use is not isolated to baseball.

Jim Sensenbrenner

Is it in the best interest of baseball to sell beer in the ninth inning? Probably not. The rule has got to be more clearly defined. And then some process should be set up where the judge is not also the appeals judge.

George Steinbrenner

As a youngster, I played in Little League, Pony League, and all sorts of amateur baseball programs growing up.

Jim Evans

It was really tough as a kid going to a Braves game. It was a guaranteed loss. You're looking at 100 losses a year. I was a huge baseball fan, played it for quite a while. But when '91 happened, with Smoltz and Glavine, it turned around, and I will say it made it pretty sweet.

Brian Baumgartner

Baseball has all the money.

Brett Hull

Many of the greatest black athletes of all time played baseball for no money and no recognition. I'm just sorry many major league fans never got to see them play, because many of them were awesome.

Monte Irvin

I'm not a fan of baseball really.

Andrew Bogut

I grew up in a small town in Illinois, and my dad was a basketball coach. Thanks to him, I have excellent fundamentals in both basketball and baseball.

Nick Offerman

I love the game of baseball.

Dusty Baker

I have gone from a player who thought he would spend his whole career with one organization to a player who's been with three organizations in a week. It's like rotisserie baseball.

Mike Piazza

If I couldn't broadcast baseball games, I think I would make a good impression on people.

Mackenzie Astin

I love the flow of the game. There's a certain fluidity to basketball. I don't enjoy watching baseball or football in the same way.

Adam Yauch

Bitcoin, in the short or even long term, may turn out be a good investment in the same way that anything that is rare can be considered valuable. Like baseball cards. Or a Picasso.

Andrew Ross Sorkin

College baseball, I love it. I love to work with the younger kids who are trying to live out their dreams, if in fact that's what they plan on doing after college to take the next step.

Roger Clemens

I tried to get a baseball movie made a couple of years ago

and I don't think it didn't happen because I was a woman, but because sports movie don't sell internationally.

Callie Khouri

I do have a family, and obviously I spend as much time as I can with them. Though even when I'm with my family, my mind tends to drift toward baseball.

Bill James

Baseball must be a great game to survive the fools who run it.

Bill Terry

If they had rankings in baseball, maybe I would have been able to do the math and figure out my chances of being a professional baseball player versus a tennis player. But that was the decision-maker for me, I just thought I was better in tennis.

Jim Courier

I was a professional baseball player from the time I was drafted out of high school in 1981 until the time I retired in

2003.

David Cone

Today baseball is currently enjoying a run of more than 14 years without interruption, a record that would have been inconceivable in the 1990s.

David Cone

One of the many things I like about baseball is how it combines individual talent and teamsmanship.

Jed S. Rakoff

I want to be part of Major League Baseball's Hall of Fame, but I don't want to be part of the kind of Hall of Fame that's based on voters' beliefs and assumptions.

Barry Bonds

I'm an expert in baseball and I don't even have a job. I'm an expert, more so than a lot of people out there. It should be my career until I'm dead. I should be one of the instructors. I think I've earned it.

Barry Bonds

I'm going to go back to the Bay Area, this is my thing, and I'm just going to open my own school of baseball. Find a facility, find a place and just teach kids. That's what I want to do.

Barry Bonds

The perception is that baseball's players' union is protecting players to use steroids and other illegal performance-enhancing drugs.

Jim Bunning

I grew up playing sports, football, basketball, baseball, everything, and acting was such a different environment and different world for me.

Cam Gigandet

In this game of baseball, you live by the sword and die by it. You hit and get hit. Remember that.

Alvin Dark

What I'd really like to give a try is cricket, because I grew up playing American baseball.

Jeremy London

I had a job on college campus. I lost that job, but on my way home I heard an inner voice that said go out for the baseball team. I was a walk-on, and I was actually petrified as a walk-on because you're not an athlete.

Lou Brock

I was playing baseball, and I tripped over first base - I'm very clumsy - and I fell and broke my wrist. That was pretty painful.

Christopher Mintz-Plasse

Baseball was the darling of all sports back then.

Marion Motley

I had started law school at Florida State University as a part-timer. I would go two quarters, and they allowed me to drop out to play baseball, and then I'd get readmitted in September. I was convinced I was going to be a lawyer and was using my baseball salary to pay my way through school.

Tony La Russa

I think the guys that get to the All-Star Game deserve a lot of credit. They deserve their opportunity to get out there and let the baseball fandom see them.

Tony La Russa

Cuba wants to get rid of a dictator, and baseball needs a dictator.

Bob Kerrey

Baseball was a chapter in my life, and now I'm excited to start another chapter as a hitting coach.

Mark McGwire

There's not a pill or an injection that's going to give me, going to give any player the hand-eye coordination to hit a baseball.

Mark McGwire

The baseball establishment is permissive about revelry.

Curt Flood

When I auditioned for 'Pitch Perfect,' I didn't know it was a singing movie. I didn't read the script. I go to the audition, and I'm like, 'Oh, it's a baseball movie.' But then I'm reading the lines, and I'm like, 'This doesn't seem like a baseball movie.'

Adam DeVine

As a kid, I used to love to play baseball and be in Little League and sleep outside with my friends and do all those kind of things.

Gary Wright

I chose to be retired. I chose to start a family. That was one of the biggest reasons I got away from the game of baseball. I wanted to start a family. I was happy.

Mark McGwire

You know, it's a different deal - throwing a football as opposed to throwing a baseball.

Drew Bledsoe

I kind of grew up with high goals for myself; I intended to play pro baseball. Growing up in Texas, Hollywood isn't much of a reality.

Josh Henderson

I played Little League baseball, but I also played basketball. Basketball was my primary sport. When you play basketball seriously, a lot of times, through the summer season, you continue playing. So that replaced me playing baseball.

Chadwick Boseman

Through SCP Auctions, the Garvey family will also continue to share our great love for baseball by donating time and dollars to youth baseball programs.

Steve Garvey

I'm just a seasonal guy. Basketball, football, baseball, boxing, golf. Give it to me all the time.

Jerry Ferrara

I had 12 years under my belt of baseball at the amateur level before I got to the big leagues.

Tom Seaver

I just played at a club in L.A. called the Baked Potato. It fits like 90 people. It's like playing somewhere in a basement in, like, Indiana or somewhere where all your friends show up. It's really fun and there's a very different energy to that than to play to 50,000 at a Tokyo baseball stadium.

Chad Smith

I went to school every day, like everyone else, and I played baseball for my high school team. I was a part of a lot of different activities outside of school.

Jesse McCartney

I enjoy being out with the fans, I enjoy talking baseball, but to get up and tell my life story... I'm not comfortable doing that.

Bruce Sutter

Anyone interested in becoming a professional umpire and becoming eligible to work in the minor leagues must attend one of the two umpire schools sanctioned by Major League Baseball.

Jim Evans

The modern era of Cape Cod baseball dawned in 1963 when the league became a showcase for the collegiate elite.

Jane Leavy

At the high school level, the coaches get these kids in revenue-driven sports and take them away from baseball. There's so much pressure on these kids to even play spring football. We need to get the African-American players back in the game, which I think would make it not only a better game, but more exciting and entertaining for everyone.

Pat Gillick

I was a ballplayer, but only for a limited time. I grew up playing in Wisconsin. It's a very sports-centric part of the country that I grew up in and I played a lot of sports, but baseball first and foremost. I played through high school. I was a middle-infielder.

Chad Harbach

I had a basketball net that my dad had put up outside. I went out there and dribbled all day long. I wanted to play basketball. Then I'd go baseball, and then I'd go to football. I remember playing football in a plowed field. I grew up going from one thing to the next wanting to play something.

Joe Gibbs

I love baseball. I love watching baseball. As a broadcaster, I get to watch the best 700 players put on the uniform year after year. That, to me, is exciting.

Bert Blyleven

I'm a big baseball fan, and I feel proprietary about the Dodgers. I'm not the owner. I'm not the manager. But I feel passionate about the decisions that they make, and I take it personally when they make decisions I don't like.

Carlton Cuse

I wish that they had the freedoms like the Japanese and the Koreans and the Mexicans and everybody else that has that freedom to come over here and play the game, because I know Cuba has a very strong baseball history.

Rafael Palmeiro

When I think about athletes, probably my favorite guest of all time among baseball players was Ted Williams.

Charlie Rose

One of the first lessons he or she learns is that in baseball anything, absolutely anything, can happen. Just two days ago as I write this, something happened that had never happened in baseball before.

John Thorn

I'm a baseball fan, but I'm not qualified to make baseball decisions, and I don't want to pretend to be.

Mark Walter

I still dream about everything I achieved. I dream about my career, dream about playing baseball, meeting so many people, traveling so much.

Tony Oliva

Back in the Eighties, I'd buy the biggest Benetton jumper I could find and would wear it long-sleeved, hanging off my shoulders, with a varsity jacket and a baseball cap on back to front with a quiff. I was the smallest boy in my class, and I looked like a reject from New Kids On The Block. Terrible.

Jamie Bamber

I've played for teams that were family-oriented organizations. They made you feel like family. The Yankees are strictly a business. Baseball is your life and everything else is secondary.

Gary Sheffield

I wanted to play baseball ever since I was 5 years old.

Allan Ray

Baseball is a team game.

Eddie Murray

For me, baseball is about, again, the team winning.

Eddie Murray

I'm proud to be here as a man that has played first base more than anybody in the game of baseball.

Eddie Murray

I chose baseball because to me baseball is the best game of all.

Dave Winfield

If I had to name the number one asset you could have for any sport I'd say speed. In baseball, all a guy with speed has to do is make contact.

Ron Fairly

In America, we have three major sports - baseball, football and basketball. They get the most coverage. Then there's things like golf which mop up most of what is left. But track and field? We are way at the bottom of the totem pole.

Maurice Greene

Kids don't learn the fundamentals of baseball at the games anymore.

Bill Lee

I think that's why I like baseball. There's something great about it - you're young, the pitcher's young and he's got this great arm, and he doesn't really realize anything about strategy.

Bruce McCulloch

One of the inspirations for my becoming a writer was the baseball board game Strat-O-Matic.

H. G. Bissinger

You can go up in the air and everything is gone. You know, you don't think about baseball. You don't think about anything. It's just something that takes you away from everyday life. I love being in a plane and looking down to see traffic on the freeway.

Cory Lidle

With one decision, Judge Sotomayor changed the entire

dispute. Her ruling rescued the 1995 baseball season and forced the parties to resume real negotiations.

David Cone

I had a great time with baseball growing up. I was lucky to grow up with it and to learn.

Nick Johnson

Charlie Finley has soured my stomach for baseball.

Vida Blue

I played baseball because I could make more money doing that than I could doing anything else.

Bill Terry

Tell me the truth - do you think I've lost my Southern accent? I feel it comes back to me only when I'm shouting at fights or at baseball games.

Cleo Moore

I would love to see as many of the black players as possible in today's Major League Baseball make every effort to go to the Negro Leagues Museum and get a first-hand view of how it all started.

Ferguson Jenkins

I just loved officiating, and I hope what I did helped make it better. That's what I tell young umpires: you can have fun. I never spent a day where going out on a baseball field didn't make me feel better.

Doug Harvey

It really came down to deciding between baseball and soccer. Soccer won out because I enjoyed it more.

Brian McBride

Arizona was the best place. I like the competition in baseball, and the football program has been great for the past five years. I think I'll be playing as a freshman in both sports, and I think I can play with them.

Terry Vaughn

No, I've never played baseball in my life.

Jay Hernandez

That's the best thing about being an actor. If you're in a baseball movie, you walk away knowing way more about baseball, or if you're in a sci-fi film, you learn way more about Comic-Con, and so I loved all that.

Topher Grace

When I'm not at work, I put deep conditioner in my hair and wear a baseball cap. I'll just roll around on the off-days with goop in my hair, and then just rinse it out.

Sarah Rafferty

My kids have played soccer and baseball and basketball, and the parents who come to games are always saying and doing things that are just wildly inappropriate.

Jeff Garlin

Imagine if these computer geeks who are running baseball now were allowed to run a war? They'd be telling our soldiers: 'That's enough. You've fired too many bullets from your rifle this week!'

Tom Seaver

I'm always telling people baseball needs to be more
prominent in the African American community. What a
better way to do so, going on these TV shows and
appearing on the cover of this or that. Now kids can see
how baseball can change your life. Frank Thomas did that
for me.

Matt Kemp

Without Cooperstown, you don't have baseball: Baseball is
history.

Brian Kilmeade

I always thought that it was kind of silly that a baseball
card could be worth so much money.

Matthew Modine

We're just being ourselves and having fun playing baseball.
The biggest thing is when people look at our team, they can
see that we're having a lot of fun.

Johnny Damon

I won an MVP trophy with the St. Louis Amateur Baseball Association. I didn't even start. I was a sub on this team. This was, like, an All-Star game where we had athletes from different teams, different mixtures. We had, like, the only black team in the league, basically. We had four players go to the All-Star game.

Nelly

I'm truly passionate about basketball. I'm not as passionate about baseball as I am about basketball, but I watch baseball and I watch football. I love sports in general.

Patrick Soon-Shiong

He really loved baseball and loved being on the field. But Mantle was lonely in a lot of ways. He had many great friends, and by all accounts was a good, generous and loyal friend. But there were a lot of people who wanted only a piece of him.

Jane Leavy

In the glory days of Orioles, when I was a newbie baseball

writer for the Post, the roster of talkers was as good as the everyday lineup. Singy - Ken Singleton - Flanny, and Cakes - the underwear spokesman Jim Palmer - were my go-to guys, occupying stalls along one wall of the shabby chic clubhouse.

Jane Leavy

All I can do is do my best work, try to create the best kind of moment to moment reality that I can do. That's what I do. I'm an actor. And all the rest of it is like baseball. You hit the ball. Sometimes it goes in the hole. Sometimes it goes to the player.

Tobin Bell

It's tempting, because as one senator said to me, 'We know if we invite baseball down, we'll draw a crowd'.

Fay Vincent

The economics of baseball are the big problem. The big clubs make a lot of money and the little clubs don't.

Fay Vincent

I think the last game console I had was Super Nintendo. I remember once I played the Sega Genesis. But Super Nintendo was my last game device. I played outside more. I liked kickball and baseball.

Natalie Martinez

I knew how to read box scores and who the baseball heroes were before I had ever seen or even heard much of a game.

W. P. Kinsella

I like getting up in front of an audience. It's fun when you go to a baseball game and the crowd is cheering you. I can't deny it. And it's very funny, too. Sometimes you're shy; you go somewhere and everyone's looking at you, so you feel a little self-conscious.

Jon Lovitz

Baseball is not a grind for me.

Steve Finley

I'm a big sports guy - golf, tennis, baseball, basketball, snowboarding - and I love games.

Jason Dohring

Marlins Park is what I call my office in Miami, because I work for the Venezuelan Museum of Baseball and Hall of Fame. My job is to go to all the MLB stadiums and to talk to and collect articles from all the Venezuelan players in the big leagues and those Americans that played in Venezuela.

Juan Pablo Galavis

I don't care what you do - baseball or politics - George W. Bush is always going to be compared to his father. I just want it to be an easy answer in 50 years - Who was the better player, me, or my kids? I want it to be my kids.

Andy Van Slyke

I'm not like a 90-mph fastball kind of guy, but I can hit 70 on radar gun. I hit 70 one time on a radar guy at one of those pitch-and-throw kind of things. I have a pretty good arm for somebody who's not a baseball player.

Ben Gibbard

I love sharing my knowledge of hitting with others. Now

coaches and players at all levels can learn my systematic approach to hitting a baseball with more consistency, mental strength and accuracy.

Dusty Baker

Watching baseball under the lights is like observing dogs indoors, at a pedigree show. In both instances, the environment is too controlled to suit the species.

Melvin Maddocks

People who think they know what they are talking about when they talk about baseball include the announcers and all of the sports press - no matter how much evidence you present them to the contrary they will continue to think that what they think is right.

Michael Lewis

My dad and all my family were into baseball. His brothers, my mom's brothers, my mom's father. Baseball was just always a part of our family.

Mark Teixeira

I started playing baseball and soccer. Those were my sports on the streets and in school when I was growing up. I didn't even start playing basketball until I was 14.

Earl Monroe

When I was in baseball and you went into the clubhouse, you didn't see ball players with curling irons.

Red Barber

In regards to core training, I try to incorporate the medicine ball whenever possible. As a baseball player, there is a lot of twisting and turning that I will do. Keeping my abs strong is as important as anything else.

Albert Pujols

My wife and I love children. We have five of our own. I would ask that anyone who looks up to me would instead look up to God. I am nothing without Him. Everything I do in life and in baseball is to glorify Him.

Albert Pujols

Baseball players practice, runners practice, so how can you

practice being funny? You get up onstage. You train as an improviser, playing make-believe, using the vernacular of improvisation, saying 'yes and' to other people's ideas, making statements.

Ali Farahnakian

My dad introduced me to baseball. Then one of my friends asked if I could play on a team; my dad said I could, and I just fell in love with the game.

Bert Blyleven

Baseball hasn't been the national pastime for many years now - no sport is. The national pastime, like it or not, is watching television.

Bob Greene

I'm not defined by baseball. I'd love for the Hall of Fame to happen, but if it doesn't, my life won't change. I'll still be coaching my boy's games.

Tom Glavine

Baseball and malaria keep coming back.

Gene Mauch

One of the things I've learned is that baseball is something that happens over time.

Mark Walter

If I go to a baseball game, I hear 'Shoeless Joe,' but otherwise, I hear 'toe pick' five times a day. No matter how many more movies I make, that'll be on my gravestone.

D. B. Sweeney

I studied Jeet Kune Do and Brazilian Jiu-Jitsu. On element of Jeet Kune Do is that I had several of years of practice with the kali stick - a stick with a size and length similar to a baseball bat.

Jose Pablo Cantillo

The debate analysis in the media is rampant with contest analogies of war, baseball, boxing, football; you name it. Any testosterone contest imaginable is fair game.

Jonathan Raymond

I wanted to be a professional baseball player.

Balthazar Getty

I wasn't ever good enough to be on the baseball team and that sort of stuff.

Balthazar Getty

I don't wish I did anything differently. The most important thing to me was to play baseball.

Eddie Murray

My message to a lot of guys is, if you like school and you like education, baseball is gonna be there, and you can get some of the same great competition in college that you do in the low minor leagues.

Barry Larkin

I played baseball in college but I didn't identify with the jocks, I was in my own little world .

Nicholas Brendon

I played softball for a few years growing up. Both my brothers played baseball.

Maggie Lawson

My first interest in baseball is the welfare of baseball itself. My second is the Cincinnati Reds, and my third is Warren Giles.

Warren Giles

I'll tell you what's helped me my entire life. I look at baseball as a game. It's something where people can go out, enjoy and have fun. Nothing more.

Harry Caray

I go to the gym in a baseball cap, sweats and then run into a boy I like. It happens - so what?

Azita Ghanizada

When I was a kid, I wanted to be a baseball player.

Takeru Kobayashi

I don't believe there's a baseball job that I couldn't take care of.

Don Cooper

Baseball, boxing, handball - sooner or later every game gets compared to narrative, but only in football are the plays perfectly linear, drawn up with letters, and only in football is the field itself lined like a sheet of notebook paper.

J. R. Moehringer

Baseball's what I do.

Bill Buckner

It was the baseball fantasy of a lifetime - to be able to sit on the bench with all those professional athletes. I got to take my son along because I wasn't sure I would be able to play with them.

Matthew Modine

John Henry Lloyd is the man I gave the credit to for polishing my skills. He taught me how to play third base and how to protect myself. John taught me more baseball than anyone else.

Judy Johnson

I know that baseball players have certain rituals or habits that they develop, because sometimes it becomes somewhat superstitious if they get on a streak and want to do the same thing over and over again.

Chadwick Boseman

I've played a baseball player a few times, but in my career I've been blessed to have played a wide range of characters.

Daniel Sunjata

Luck is the great stabilizer in baseball.

Tris Speaker

I was planning to be a baseball player until I ran into something called a curveball. And that set me back.

Ben Chandler

The genius of our institutions is democratic - baseball is a democratic game.

Al Spalding

Two hours is about as long as any American can wait for the close of a baseball game, or anything else for that matter.

Al Spalding

It's very warm there, so we were outdoors all the time. The local people had programs for us year-round, where as kids we had the opportunity to play football, basketball, baseball, track and field - we just went from one sport to the next, year-round.

Rafer Johnson

I grew up playing hockey and baseball, so I wish I had time to get back into it, but living in L.A. and North Carolina, you have to take advantage of the golf.

Diego Klattenhoff

Baseball fans! Good lord! I feel like sports fans get mad at you easier than country music fans. It scares me. I'm glad that country fans don't get mad every time I mess up.

Ashley Monroe

I'm a Baltimore guy. I've always loved Baltimore and always will love Baltimore, but baseball is baseball, and when you're playing on the opposing team, you're going to get booed.

Mark Teixeira

I've worked in supermarkets, put tags in baseball caps and provided security during Wimbledon, but I never thought acting would be something I'd be any good at, or make a living from.

Claire Foy

When I started playing the game of baseball, the more I played and the better numbers I got, the more I started thinking about the Hall of Fame. But I never thought I had a chance to be there.

Roberto Alomar

I'm just a poor boy from the cornfields of Richmond, Virginia. I'm proud because I loved baseball and played with the best.

Ray Dandridge

Seven is more than a lucky number or a famous baseball player's uniform. It's the brain's natural shepherd, herding vast amounts of information into manageable chunks.

Jacqueline Leo

If you've ever been around a group of actors, you've noticed, no doubt, that they can talk of nothing else under the sun but acting. It's exactly the same way with baseball players. Your heart must be in your work.

Christy Mathewson

I love both sports, but the deciding factor was, being a left-handed pitcher, I had a huge advantage in baseball because of that, and I didn't have that type of advantage in hockey.

Tom Glavine

If you're giving me tickets to the football game, baseball

game or hockey game, I'm taking the tickets to the hockey game. For me, it's by far the most fun sport to go and watch live and be part of. I just don't know why it doesn't translate as well on TV.

Tom Glavine

In Boston I got to a point where I thought I was putting out fires more than being a baseball coach. And some of it was my fault. I was getting stubborn. My fuse was a little shorter than it needed to be. And that helps nobody.

Terry Francona

I played baseball in college, and then I went to Russia to study acting and played some pro ball over there.

Jon Bernthal

I am through with baseball forever. I have my farm and my home and enough to take care of me, so why should I work and worry any longer?

Eddie Plank

I sing the 'Star Spangled Banner,' so I can get into football, basketball and baseball games for free.

John Cullum

As I look out there and see the culture of baseball, a lot of blacks and Latins, it's given me a lot of joy to know that Jackie started that. If Jackie hadn't come in '47, me and Ron Santo wouldn't have played in Double-A and all those years in the big leagues.

Billy Williams

You never really know baseball until you put on a pair of cleats and get out and play it; and if you play for five years, you still don't really know what it's about.

Waite Hoyt

Baseball's my life.

Justin Verlander

I had no other interests but baseball because I never thought I'd not make it. No. Never.

Justin Verlander

I owe baseball all that I have and much of what I hope to have. Baseball made my entrance to the film industry immeasurably easier than I could have made it alone. To the greatest game in the world I shall be eternally in debt.

Chuck Connors

The day I left baseball, I became smart. When I was in baseball, I played for the love of the game. I'd sign any contract they gave me. But then I stopped playing and began doing interviews with the players at the ball park. I began to see the light.

Chuck Connors

I played a lot of baseball growing up, and I always hit better if I kept moving before the pitch instead of standing still in the batter's box. I think a waggle does the same thing in the golf swing. It keeps you relaxed and gets your body ready to hit the ball.

Jason Dufner

There are no war stories. I ended up a bombardier, but I never got overseas. And it wasn't because I was playing baseball either. It was just a series of things that went on.

Bobby Thomson

The difference between a home run and a swing-and-a-miss is, what, an inch and a half? You can throw a great pitch, the guy makes a great swing. And if it's at a guy, it's an out. That's the beauty of baseball, really. There's not just one guy in control.

Phil Humber

If it wasn't for baseball, I'd be in either the penitentiary or the cemetery.

Babe Ruth

I knew when my career was over. In 1965 my baseball card came out with no picture.

Bob Uecker

The great trouble with baseball today is that most of the players are in the game for the money and that's it, not for the love of it, the excitement of it, the thrill of it.

Ty Cobb

The only thing I can do is play baseball. I have to play ball. It's the only thing I know.

Mickey Mantle

I became a soldier, not because I had a military vocation initially, but because it was the only way that that young, poor-class child from the provinces could go to the center of the country: through baseball, which was my dream.

Hugo Chavez

You don't have to know anything about baseball to respond to Babe Ruth because he's just this magnificent human being. And a really good story because he was this kid who grew up essentially as an orphan, you know, had a tough life, and then he became the most successful baseball player ever. But he was also a really good guy.

Bill Bryson

Close don't count in baseball. Close only counts in horseshoes and grenades.

Frank Robinson

No baseball pitcher would be worth a darn without a catcher who could handle the hot fastball.

Casey Stengel

In baseball, you can't kill the clock. You've got to give the other man his chance. That's why this is the greatest game.

Earl Weaver

Jimmy Carter was - he still - he remains to this day America's most ex of ex-presidents. You just can't believe that we elected this doofus. He was a bright enough guy and sort of well-meaning. But he was about as prepared to be president of the United States as your goofy old uncle, you know, the one that memorises baseball statistics.

P. J. O'Rourke

I think about baseball when I wake up in the morning. I think about it all day and I dream about it at night. The only time I don't think about it is when I'm playing it.

Carl Yastrzemski

Baseball, it is said, is only a game. True. And the Grand

Canyon is only a hole in Arizona. Not all holes, or games, are created equal.

George Will

I love to play baseball. I'm a baseball player. I've always been a baseball player. I'm still a baseball player. That's who I am.

Ryne Sandberg

If you have a bad day in baseball, and start thinking about it, you will have 10 more.

Sammy Sosa

I've always wanted to be the best in the world as a baseball player, so when I started to think about opening a business, it was with that mindset.

Curt Schilling

You know that everyone thinks that in order to do South Park we must be wild, crazy, rock and roll stars. But the truth is we're just wholesome middle-American guys. We enjoy soda pop, baseball and beating up old people just as much as anybody.

Trey Parker

When we played the Dodgers in St. Louis, they had to come through our dugout, and our bat rack was right there where they had to walk. My bats kept disappearing, and I couldn't figure it out. Turns out, Pee Wee Reese was stealing my bats. I found that out later, after we got out of baseball. He and Rube Walker stole my bats.

Stan Musial

Until my senior year, baseball and basketball were my best sports; and even when I was a senior, I still wanted to play baseball professionally. But the family wanted me to go to college, and I guess I agreed with them, or else I would have accepted some of the offers I got.

Joe Namath

Baseball has the great advantage over cricket of being sooner ended.

George Bernard Shaw

Like a baseball game, wars are not over till they are over. Wars don't run on a clock like football. No previous generation was so hopelessly unrealistic that this had to be explained to them.

Thomas Sowell

Now there's three things you can do in a baseball game: You can win or you can lose or it can rain.

Casey Stengel

My father kept me busy from dawn to dusk when I was a kid. When I wasn't pitching hay, hauling corn or running a tractor, I was heaving a baseball into his mitt behind the barn... If all the parents in the country followed his rule, juvenile delinquency would be cut in half in a year's time.

Bob Feller

Baseball is like driving, it's the one who gets home safely that counts.

Tommy Lasorda

I'm a terrible singer. I feel lucky to play baseball. You can't be gifted in everything.

Alex Rodriguez

I'd rather be a good person off the field than a good baseball player on the field.

Bryce Harper

I only had one player in my 33 years of sports that couldn't be traded. He wore No. 23 - and 45 when he played baseball.

Jerry Reinsdorf

Nobody gets any fun out of baseball any more. I guess a kid's crazy not to be serious about it when he's drawing down $20,000 or $30,000 a year, and any smart-aleck gag you try may be your last. But what's life without a laugh?

Rabbit Maranville

I'm among the first girls ever to play Little League baseball, and to my knowledge, the very first in western Illinois. It was 1976, and I was a nine-year-old tomboy whose older brothers had played.

Therese Fowler

I've been lucky. I've met a lot of baseball people, and I've learned to value people who talk - people who talk well and in long sentences and even long paragraphs.

Roger Angell

Baseball cannot be learned as a trade. It begins with the sport of the schoolboy, and though it may end in the professional, I am sure there is not a single one of these who learned the game with the expectation of making it a business. There have been years in the life of each during which he must have ate and drank and dreamed baseball.

John Montgomery Ward

In the field of outdoor sports, the American boy is easily capable of devising his own amusements, and until some proof is adduced that baseball is not his invention, I protest against this systematic effort to rob him of his dues.

John Montgomery Ward

The Capone era. That was my time. Capone was a big baseball fan. He'd walk into the ballpark like the president walking in today, with bodyguards all around him.

Billy Herman

When I started in professional baseball, I had what you might call a rude awakening. See this scar right next to my left ear? That's where the pitcher hit me the very first time I came to bat as a pro. I was out cold for about 10 minutes.

Billy Herman

I moved on from dice baseball to 'MLB: The Show' on PlayStation.

Nate Corddry

The big tragedy in baseball is that the amateur spirit has gone out of it to a large extent.

Larry MacPhail

My dad was my coach in baseball and early on in basketball, so playing baseball was something we always did.

Matthew Stafford

Growing up, I played 'Ken Griffey, Jr. Baseball' and just whatever I could get my hands on. When I was really young, I was a big fan of Mario and that type of stuff. I still play videogames now, so it was really cool for me to be able to play as myself on '2K6' or '2K7,' I believe it was, when I was a rookie.

Justin Verlander

I remember wearing the big oversized baseball and basketball jerseys and Timbaland boots. I was a tomboy growing up. I recently caught a picture of myself, and I was like, 'God! What was I thinking about?'

Drew Sidora

I was a big baseball player, and my passion in life, in third grade, was collecting baseball cards. That was my childhood thing.

Alan Ritchson

What's odd is that nobody in my family is an artist. My cousins are, like, secretaries at law firms or nurses or just more blue collar. And I was in a baseball team. I used to be, like, a really big tomboy.

Melonie Diaz

Going home and just seeing what a mess youth baseball was was an eye-opener. I just want to make it a better game.

Roy Halladay

I enjoy talking pitching and talking baseball. And I don't have all the answers. I don't claim to, but I'm more than happy to share my beliefs.

Roy Halladay

Nothing in baseball can bring me down to the level where I was growing up in Pine Bluff, crying and broke. This is fun for me. Whenever you see me slumping, nah, I don't get upset; I'm all right.

Torii Hunter

I played baseball as a left-handed first baseman, though never as well as I did quarterbacking.

Bob Sheppard

The fact is, when I was 15 and a sophomore at high school, I played on the varsity baseball team for the college.

Johnny Mize

I was a baseball guy. Mom wouldn't let me play football when I was little because she was scared I'd get hurt. So, I finally convinced her to let me play in 7th grade.

Calvin Johnson

It wasn't really until the 10th or 11th grade when I started to play well, and football took the place of baseball, which was my love when I was five years old. I don't know what happened; baseball just got boring to me, I guess.

Calvin Johnson

My friends like to play as me in the baseball games, and they call to tell me about every bag I steal. And you know, every time a new game comes out, I check to make sure my speed is up to par. But to me, when you talk video games, you're talking 'Madden.'

Carl Crawford

For me, baseball just brings up a lot of nostalgic, happy feelings because I enjoyed it as a kid, and I liked being out there playing in the sun, and it was a simpler time for all of us.

Robert Lorenz

I just got hooked on the radio, the voice of it all. It was my connection to metropolitan America, if you will. Sports, in particularly baseball then 'cause of its rich sediment of numbers, was one of the first things a young person could peg up with adults on - that is, you could know as much about Jimmy Fox as your father did.

George Will

You can't be afraid to make errors! You can't be afraid to be naked before the crowd, because no one can ever master the game of baseball, or conquer it. You can only challenge it.

Lou Brock

I'm human and I've played my butt off for ten years. I'm not a loafer, I'm not a jerk, I'm a baseball player.

Reggie Jackson

Imagine if you had baseball cards that showed all the performance stats for your people: batting averages, home runs, errors, ERAs, win/loss records. You could see what they did well and poorly and call on the right people to play the right positions in a very transparent way.

Ray Dalio

When I started to sing, my mother would have me engaged to perform at the Women's Christian Temperance Union national or annual meetings. I would hate doing this because I wanted to play baseball or go off skiing.

Maureen Forrester

In baseball you have individual responsibility, and if you fail it, you get an error. But at the same time, your focus is on the common goal of the team to win. This is part of what resonates with people about baseball. This is how they would like society to work.

Jed S. Rakoff

My dad's a bodybuilder. My whole life I've been taught to train the hard way. I believe in earning strength, not buying it. My grandfather raised me old school: In baseball, you work for whatever you get.

Gary Sheffield

Since I was in high school, I wanted to play professional football and professional baseball, be a two-sport star.

Russell Wilson

Other kids went out and beat each other up or played baseball, and I built electronics.

Robert Moog

Kids are our future, and we hope baseball has given them some idea of what it is to live together and how we can get along, whether you be black or white.

Larry Doby

Poets are like baseball pitchers. Both have their moments. The intervals are the tough things.

Robert Frost

A baseball game is simply a nervous breakdown divided into nine innings.

Earl Wilson

Some say our national pastime is baseball. Not me. It's gossip.

Erma Bombeck

Opera in English is, in the main, just about as sensible as baseball in Italian.

H. L. Mencken

Baseball changes through the years. It gets milder.

Babe Ruth

The key to winning baseball games is pitching, fundamentals, and three run homers.

Earl Weaver

These old ballparks are like cathedrals in America. We

don't have big old Gothic cathedrals like they do in Europe. But we got baseball parks.

Jimmy Buffett

There are three things you can do in a baseball game. You can win, or you can lose, or it can rain.

Casey Stengel

Well, baseball was my whole life. Nothing's ever been as fun as baseball.

Mickey Mantle

Let the teachers teach English and I will teach baseball. There is a lot of people in the United States who say isn't, and they ain't eating.

Dizzy Dean

I admitted I bet on baseball, but I wasn't suspended from baseball for betting on baseball.

Pete Rose

It was all I lived for, to play baseball.

Mickey Mantle

It's a wonderful feeling to be a bridge to the past and to unite generations. The sport of baseball does that, and I am just a part of it.

Vin Scully

I really love baseball. The guys and the game, and I love the challenge of describing things. The only thing I hate - and I know you have to be realistic and pay the bills in this life - is the loneliness on the road.

Vin Scully

I think I could have become an outstanding professional baseball player, but I don't think I could have reached the heights that I have in football - being one of the very top players in the game, being a world champion.

Joe Namath

Thank you... adjustable baseball caps with no logo on the front and mesh netting in the back, for being a great way to say, 'Hi, I'm over 80 years old.'

Jimmy Fallon

My kid was a great baseball player. I thought I had it made. Front-row seats at Yankee Stadium. Then he turned sixteen and wanted to be a rapper.

James Caan

Don't try to tell Namath's people on First Avenue about Babe Ruth, because they don't even know the name. In fact, with the young, you can forget all of baseball. The sport is gone. But if you ever have seen Ruth, and then you see Namath, you know there is very little difference.

Jimmy Breslin

I came up in 1941 and I played against men who played in the 1930s. I stayed until 1963 playing against men who will be playing in the 1970s. So I think I can feel qualified to say that baseball really was a great game, and baseball is really a great game, and baseball will always be a great game.

Stan Musial

I'm a very lucky guy. I had so many people help me over the years that I never had many problems. If I had a problem, I could sit down with someone and they would explain the problem to me, and the problem become like a baseball game.

Willie Mays

All these fifty-year-old guys wearing baseball caps and shorts and acting like children. It winds me up. Men don't have to take responsibility anymore. Most of the guys I know would punch me on the nose for saying this, but maybe we do have to bring back conscription.

Chrissie Hynde

I always thought that there was going to be life after baseball, and so I designed that in my life I would have other interests after baseball that I would be able to step into. And I didn't realize the grip that baseball had on me and on my family.

Nolan Ryan

It really gets into your system. All baseball players have this internal clock around February when it starts to kick in and the juices start to flow. I think underestimated how much I was going to miss it.

David Cone

A catcher must want to catch. He must make up his mind that it isn't the terrible job it is painted, and that he isn't going to say every day, 'Why, oh why with so many other positions in baseball did I take up this one.'

Bill Dickey

I knew I was the second-best tennis player in the state of Florida and No. 8 in the United States of America when I was 12 years old and I couldn't tell you what I was in baseball, but I liked my chances in tennis of getting a scholarship to college.

Jim Courier

No matter how much technology changes scouting, no matter how much free agency and big TV contracts change the business of baseball, I hope and pray that the heart of the game will never change.

Pat Gillick

It's fun; baseball's fun.

Yogi Berra

In baseball, you don't know nothing.

Yogi Berra

If it weren't for baseball, many kids wouldn't know what a millionaire looked like.

Phyllis Diller

Being with a woman all night never hurt no professional baseball player. It's staying up all night looking for a woman that does him in.

Casey Stengel

Opening day. All you have to do is say the words and you feel the shutters thrown wide, the room air out, the light pour in. In baseball, no other day is so pure with possibility. No scores yet, no losses, no blame or disappointment. No hangover, at least until the game's over.

Mary Schmich

The first books I was interested in were all about baseball. But I can't think of one single book that changed my life in any way.

Charles Kuralt

I ain't ever had a job, I just always played baseball.

Satchel Paige

Going out and playing football or baseball with the boys, when I was a tomboy, was a great way to learn about winning and losing, and most girls didn't have that experience.

Hillary Clinton

When you're mad at someone, it's probably best not to break his arm with a baseball bat.

Evel Knievel

If you're playing baseball and thinking about managing, you're crazy. You'd be better off thinking about being an owner.

Casey Stengel

Richard Schiff is a really good baseball player. It's surprising because he looks exhausted.

Bradley Whitford

Baseball is almost the only orderly thing in a very unorderly world. If you get three strikes, even the best lawyer in the world can't get you off.

Bill Veeck

My mom, she wasn't like a baseball mother who knew everything about the game. She just wanted me to be happy with what I was doing.

David Ortiz

Now that women are jockeys, baseball umpires, atomic scientists, and business executives, maybe someday they can master parallel parking.

Bill Vaughan

You spend a good piece of your life gripping a baseball and in the end it turns out that it was the other way around all the time.

Jim Bouton

Baseball for me was instinctive, born within me, given to me as a gift from God.

Willie Stargell

Making love is like hitting a baseball. You just gotta relax and concentrate.

Susan Sarandon

In baseball, democracy shines its clearest. The only race that matters is the race to the bag. The creed is the rule book. And color, merely something to distinguish one team's uniform from another's.

Ernie Harwell

I'm a football guy. Baseball, I enjoy it at playoff time.

Jon Bon Jovi

The triple is the most exciting play in baseball. Home runs win a lot of games, but I never understood why fans are so obsessed with them.

Hank Aaron

Baseball is a tongue-tied kid from Georgia growing up to be an announcer and praising the Lord for showing him the way to Cooperstown. This is a game for America. Still a game for America, this baseball!

Ernie Harwell

Every player should be accorded the privilege of at least one season with the Chicago Cubs. That's baseball as it should be played - in God's own sunshine. And that's really living.

Alvin Dark

Baseball is more than a game. It's like life played out on a field.

Juliana Hatfield

The content and thematic materials of dance is, of itself,

like boxing. You play tennis and baseball. But boxing is not a sport you play: you stand up and do it.

Twyla Tharp

President Bush left for Canada today to attend a trade summit. Reportedly, the trade summit got off to an awkward start when the president pulled out his baseball cards.

Conan O'Brien

I like to see the difference between good and evil as kind of like the foul line at a baseball game. It's very thin, it's made of something very flimsy like lime, and if you cross it, it really starts to blur where fair becomes foul and foul becomes fair.

Harlan Coben

Baseball is not a sport you can achieve individually.

Curt Schilling

I could have played another year, but I would have been playing for the money, and baseball deserves better than that.

George Brett

Now, I know you expected me to say that, well, I just kick back in the rocking chair, fished a little bit, listened to Willie Nelson tapes and watched old baseball games on the Classic Sports network. And, tell you the truth, I have done that for maybe about five total minutes.

Dan Rather

For me, baseball is the most nourishing game outside of literature. They both are re-tellings of human experience.

A. Bartlett Giamatti

Baseball just a came as simple as a ball and bat. Yet, as complex as the American spirit it symbolizes. A sport, a business and sometimes almost even a religion.

Ernie Harwell

Not everybody's a baseball fan.

Derek Jeter

The first thing to know about playing baseball in Michigan is, Michigan's really cold.

Derek Jeter

I have observed that baseball is not unlike a war, and when you come right down to it, we batters are the heavy artillery.

Ty Cobb

Baseball hasn't forgotten me. I go to a lot of old-timers games and I haven't lost a thing. I sit in the bullpen and let people throw things at me. Just like old times.

Bob Uecker

When I was growing up, there weren't any Little Leagues in the city. Parents worked all the time. They didn't have time to take their kids out to play baseball and football.

Mike Krzyzewski

As American as an apple is and as American as baseball is, they don't go together. You can't be chewing an apple at a baseball game. You've got to let go of the diet that day.

Kevin James

As far as I'm concerned, Aaron is the best ball player of my era. He is to baseball of the last fifteen years what Joe DiMaggio was before him. He's never received the credit he's due.

Mickey Mantle

To me, baseball has always been a reflection of life. Like life, it adjusts. It survives everything.

Willie Stargell

My first and only experience in baseball, the coach signed me up; he didn't tell me there's a thing called the curveball. I didn't know that. So the ball's coming at me and I start backing out, and then it broke inside. And the umpire says, 'Strike one!' And I'm saying, 'How is that a strike? It almost hit me!'

Magic Johnson

Sport is a wonderful metaphor for life. Of all the sports that

I played - skiing, baseball, fishing - there is no greater example than golf, because you're playing against yourself and nature.

Robert Redford

I started skating and I kind of liked it because I could run circles around the guys that wouldn't pick me to play baseball.

Scott Hamilton

Now, modern economies have a very effective mechanism for deciding if salaries are really too high: it's called the free market. That's how most people's salaries are set, after all, including those of major-league baseball players and European soccer players.

James Surowiecki

Everything I have, I owe to baseball and the Dodgers.

Tommy Lasorda

Baseball has been very good to me.

Roberto Clemente

I guess my thermometer for my baseball fever is still a goose bump.

Vin Scully

I'm not much interested in sport just as sport. I wouldn't be interested in making a golf film or baseball or fishing film.

Robert Redford

The number one priority is playing baseball. There are so many people in New York trying to get you to do this and get you to do that, which is fine, but you have to take care of yourself.

Derek Jeter

I know a baseball star who wouldn't report the theft of his wife's credit cards because the thief spends less than she does.

Joe Garagiola

Baseball is an individual game, but it should never be a personal game.

Pete Rose

As a kid, before I could play music, I remember baseball being the one thing that could always make me happy.

Garth Brooks

I tried golf for a while, but I wasn't very good at it, so I didn't play a lot of golf. I enjoy all sports, not just football. I like basketball, baseball, and I got into the World Cup. So really, sports in general are my life, and football specifically.

John Madden

I found myself in a race with Mother Nature to play as much baseball as I could before she forced me to stop.

Willie Stargell

Baseball is only a game, a game of inches and a lot of luck. During a time of all-out war, sports are very insignificant.

Bob Feller

Growing up, I actually wanted to be a professional baseball player instead of a radio DJ. Believe it or not.

Casey Kasem

Baseball life is a tough life on the family.

Nolan Ryan

I think I was the best baseball player I ever saw.

Willie Mays

Baseball's future? Bigger and bigger, better and better! No question about it, it's the greatest game there is!

Ted Williams

Baseball is a spirited race of man against man, reflex against reflex. A game of inches. Every skill is measured. Every heroic, every failing is seen and cheered, or booed. And then becomes a statistic.

Ernie Harwell

People know more about baseball players' contracts than they do about the policies that govern the fate of our children's lives in twenty years. Think about it. People used to say, the whole time I was growing up, 'Do you want to bring a child into this world?' That's pretty dire.

Jackson Browne

I am so happy and proud to learn of Hideo Nomo's election to the Japanese Baseball Hall of Fame. He was quite a pitcher and competitor, but he is also a very special and caring person.

Tommy Lasorda

Whenever I wasn't watching the planes, I was playing community baseball, football, or something like that.

Bo Jackson

Why the fairy tale of Willie Mays making a brilliant World Series catch, and then dashing off to play stickball in the street with his teenage pals. That's baseball. So is the husky voice of a doomed Lou Gehrig saying, 'I consider myself the luckiest man on the face of this earth.'

Ernie Harwell

Baseball was one-hundred percent of my life.

Ty Cobb

The interesting thing is that it seems like George W. Bush would have been happy being the president of anything. He could have been president of Major League Baseball.

Eddie Vedder

There's a man in Mobile who remembers that Honus Wagner hit a triple in Pittsburgh 46 years ago. That's baseball.

Ernie Harwell

As a member of Congress, I'm often reminded that in baseball, as in diplomacy, you have to know when to hit, when to run, and when to show grace.

Linda Sanchez

I love the game, it's the greatest game on earth, that's why I can't understand all of this talk about trying to make the game better. People talk about the high strike zone and changing this and that. Why? To speed up the game? That's the beauty of baseball. There is no time element.

Eric Davis

You can talk about teamwork on a baseball team, but I'll tell you, it takes teamwork when you have 2,900 men stationed on the U.S.S. Alabama in the South Pacific.

Bob Feller

The game of baseball is better when the Dodgers are playing well, just like when the Yankees are playing well, or the Cubs, the Phillies, the big-name teams.

Pete Rose

Baseball calls it a curve ball for a reason: you just don't know where some pitches will land. Your ace could get injured. Your golden glover could err. Your team could sit through a rain delay. Your manager could get ejected. Your bench must be broad and deep enough to overcome.

Christine Pelosi

Hats have been my thing pretty much my whole life but

finance has not. I would go to the corner store and buy really cheap baseball style caps and wear those to school.

Ne-Yo

Now, you tell me, if I have a day off during the baseball season, where do you think I'll spend it? The ballpark. I still love it. Always have, always will.

Harry Caray

Baseball and the players association have rules. If you stay within the rules - which say that you can play while you're appealing - I don't see what anyone would be in arms about.

Pete Rose

In baseball, I was always in control of everything until I let the ball go.

Curt Schilling

When I won the world championship, in 1972, the United States had an image of, you know, a football country, a baseball country, but nobody thought of it as an intellectual country.

Bobby Fischer

I can wear a baseball cap; I am entitled to wear a baseball cap. I am genetically pre-disposed to wear a baseball cap, whereas most English people look wrong in a baseball cap.

Bill Bryson

In 2002, in this country, there was an observation that for the first time in America, more kids were actively pursuing skateboarding than baseball.

Stephen Baldwin

Any teammate of mine that had a kid and a boy that was capable of playing baseball, I think I set a terrific example of 'Don't do this' and 'Don't do that.' And that's one of the things that I'm most proud of.

Bob Uecker

Baseball and American football and hockey are all ahead because they have a history. The MLS is kind of new. So hopefully, in time, and with players coming and trying to develop the game, and the U.S. team also doing well - at the last World Cup, they finished above England and created some buzz.

Thierry Henry

Short of baseball and my family, it was gaming. And gaming is a $20-million to $200-million multi-year effort. It's an insane, stupid and utterly irresponsible act. But I did it.

Curt Schilling

I was always active - I went from baseball to football. I didn't have time to work out.

Bo Jackson

You need to have camaraderie in the clubhouse. Wherever you're working, be it a baseball team or at a business, you want to walk in there and say, 'Geez, it's great to be at work. Let's go get 'em,' as opposed to walking in there knowing there's going to be a commotion.

Pat Gillick

Bunting is usually a waste of time. The - generally, yeah, I mean, if you think about it, bunt is the only play in baseball that both sides applaud. The - if the home team bunts, you get a base. The home team applauds because they get an out, and the other team applauds because they get a base. So what does that tell you?

Bill James

When I began playing the game, baseball was about as gentlemanly as a kick in the crotch.

Ty Cobb

I never ride just to ride. I ride to catch a fox. I play baseball to make the team.

Sargent Shriver

You know, I'm from Boston, and in Boston, you are born with a baseball bat in your hand.

Eli Roth

In baseball, there's always the next day.

Ryne Sandberg

I had the pleasure, as Robin said, to live a childhood dream as many young Americans and Puerto Rican children live that play youth baseball. And I feel honored and very thankful for that opportunity.

Nolan Ryan